A CURIOUS HEART

THE LIFE & LETTERS OF ELIZABETH BOATWRIGHT COKER

Penelope Coker Hall and Eliza Wilson Ingle
edited by **Virginia Christian Beach**

EVENING POST BOOKS

Published by
Evening Post Books
Charleston, South Carolina

First edition

Authors: Penelope Coker Hall and Eliza Wilson Ingle
Edited by: Virginia Christian Beach
EPB Managing Editor: Jacob Hollifield
Designer: Gill Guerry

First printing 2024
Printed in the United States of America

A CIP catalog record for this book has been applied for from the Library of Congress.

ISBN: 979-8-9909493-0-0

For those who came
before and after,
who believe in the blessed
balm of laughter

CONTENTS

Elizabeth and Tom Johnson at her induction into
the South Carolina Academy of Authors.

FOREWORD

I recall for the mere delight of recalling, happenings and people that I can never forget, treasures of my curious and secret heart.

– Elizabeth Boatwright Coker

The late Elizabeth Boatwright Coker (1909-1993) – sometimes referred to affectionately as "EBC" by family and friends – was a supremely intelligent, blithe, Southern woman of charm and good humor. She is remembered and celebrated for her smart and winsome self, her many and varied accomplishments, and her lifelong commitment to South Carolina and its people. It was Elizabeth Coker's bold professional achievement as a writer and cultural force that earned her the title of "South Carolina's First Lady of Letters."

Her daughter, Penelope Coker Hall, and granddaughter Eliza Wilson Ingle have done all of us who knew EBC, and the reading public at large, a great favor in assembling such a rich and broad selection of passages from the author's personal papers, weaving them into a captivating biography. Their intimate knowledge of EBC as a mother and grandmother, and their sensitivity to and appreciation for her career as a bestselling writer, have inspired Penelope and Eliza to tell much of the author's story in her own words, thus making this volume as much EBC's as theirs – the 10th and final major book of her oeuvre.

When the time came to choose a few succinct words for the title, *A Curious Heart,* the obvious desire was to find them among EBC's own utterances. A number of appropriate possibilities revealed themselves. But a few words in particular kept asserting their perfect suitability, found among the acceptance remarks she made upon her induction into the South Carolina Hall of Fame: "I recall for the mere delight of recalling, happenings and people that I can never forget, treasures of my curious and secret heart."

• • • • •

Elizabeth Coker was indeed a woman of heart. Upon examination of her life and work, it seems that matters of the heart – love in all of its manifestations – was what may have been of ultimate value to her and the power behind her motivation. Her daughter and granddaughter confirm as much when they write, "Ultimately love – receiving it and giving it – was the basis of her indefatigable strength and boundless tolerance, her 'strongest credo.'"

First and foremost, EBC loved people. She exuded passion and compassion, and would have found these terms completely complementary. Of course, she loved family, in all of its immediate and complex connections, present and past. But she also loved the persons in her wider world: close friends and associates, casual acquaintances, and groups and classes of people whose lives touched her own in some way – average working folks, educators and students, writers and readers and researchers, business people and corporate personnel, organizational and institutional leaders.

Moreover, the innumerable less fortunate persons she encountered and assisted during her lifetime were never far from mind. Growing up in Darlington and living her adult life in Hartsville, South Carolina, she enjoyed a world of relative wealth and privilege. But EBC had experienced enough hardship and loss in her life to enable her to sympathize with those afflicted or victimized by a wide range of difficult, chronic conditions – from poverty and illness to neglect, disadvantage, injustice. Her empathy for them was expressed through various "love-in-action" measures, implemented in quiet, unheralded and sometimes secretive ways.

• • • • •

Graced by such a heart, and driven by an innate curiosity and inquiring mind, is it any wonder that a young Darlington girl named Elizabeth Boatwright should have felt compelled to put on paper what she was observing, learning and feeling? She would later say as a newly married woman, "I always wanted to be a writer." Later still: "I find it essential to write whether I have an inspiration or whether I don't." And finally: "I write whenever it is physically possible."

In fact, EBC succeeded early in becoming a published writer, with her modest appearances in print first occurring during high school and college. These were principally poems, a literary form she would employ and enjoy for the rest of her life.

Following her marriage to young South Carolina industrialist James Lide Coker III in 1930, EBC continued to write when and where time allowed, juggling her responsibilities as wife, mother and citizen. She described her life over the next 20 years as divided into "the three me's: corporate wife, doting mother and closet writer." Being a responsible wife and mother came first in the 1930s and 40s. Writing had to be a third priority. But she never stopped, publishing here and there as poet, essayist and short story writer.

Then on October 20, 1950 after decades of determined effort practicing her beloved art and craft, it happened. Elizabeth Boatwright Coker, age 41, finally saw her name on the cover of a book. At midlife and mid-century, her novel *Daughter of Strangers* was published by E. P. Dutton and Company of New York. It was her first book and would be her longest – dedicated to Jim and soon to become a *New York Times* bestseller. Years later, a first edition copy turned up in a Vermont bookshop with the following inscription: "Liz Coker Her First Book." Some say it was her best.

In a 1950 interview with Walter Spearman – fellow South Carolinian and University of North Carolina journalism professor – EBC revealed that she got the idea for *Daughter of Strangers* from an African American she knew in South Carolina "who was having great difficulties in making adjustments to the segregated life after having served in the army in England, where he found no discrimination on account of race." She goes on to say that one of the principal themes of the book was that "we must not be so bound by the traditions of our ancestors that we refuse to face the problems of our own day and continue injustices to a minority race simply because we inherited them [the injustices] from the past." This novel, inspired by a sympathetic conversation on race relations with a young Black army veteran, would change the trajectory of Elizabeth's life and work.

• • • • •

In addition to people, EBC loved many things, especially books. As a self-described "gluttonous reader," she was no doubt familiar with the great English and European novelists of the 19th century: Jane Austen, George Eliot, the Brontë sisters, Thomas Hardy, Charles Dickens and Anthony Trollope. Penelope and Eliza reveal what she once said about some of her favorite authors: "Writers of narrative imaginative stories based on believable human beings have probably been my greatest influences, such as Tolstoy, Balzac, Flaubert . . ." This was the company she no doubt wished her own novels to keep, and the quality of whose work she desired to emulate.

A devout reader of nonfiction too, EBC studied history across all continents and time periods. She assembled a host of contemporary and antiquarian works of historical writing and took pride in her collection, relying on it and other libraries across the globe for research. One of the last volumes to leave her large personal library in Hartsville was a copy of *Memoirs of Hadrian,* by the French author Marguerite Yourcenar, a contemporary of Elizabeth and the first woman to be elected to the Académie française.

No doubt EBC absorbed an enormous amount of oral history growing up. Born less than half a century following the end of the Civil War, she would have heard stories from and about members of her own South Carolina family who experienced the conflict – whether on the battlefield or at home. In a 1979 commencement address at her alma mater, Converse College, she declared: "I grew up on stories about these people and their descendants – the laughter and tears and failures and triumphs that carried them through the generations." It should come as no surprise that much of her fiction is situated in the time and places (largely Southern) defined by that bloody and tragic, but highly dramatic and fascinating period of American history.

• • • • •

EBC also loved beauty. Beauty in all its dimensions and manifestations – wherever it could be found, exhibited and expressed. Like the gift of humor that Elizabeth loved and depended upon, beauty could sometimes save the day and cover a multitude of sins. Beauty appealed to her curiosity and found endless expression in her writings.

She herself was a woman of exceptional beauty. One journalist called EBC "chic" and described her as "a glamorous, soft-spoken Southerner who looks more like Scarlet O'Hara than a reformer determined to 'undermine' the ancient traditions of the South." Publisher, editor and friend Jonathan Daniels sensed a more ethereal, lyrical quality about the author, saying that "she keeps wonder wherever she moves. Stardust and daydreams are never long absent from her great big sleepy blue eyes."

At the same time, EBC would have understood true beauty as also incorporating an essential inner human dimension. She loved and appreciated a large array of people. She no doubt saw and recognized in many of them a certain interior or spiritual beauty, manifested in such human qualities as intellectual and emotional vigor, quiet strength and resolve, generosity of spirit, deep powers of perception and self-awareness, creative energy and imagination, fortitude, kindness, compassion, forbearance, patience, humility – and always a sense of curiosity and discovery, of good humor and lightness of being. Inasmuch as her books are novels of manners – studies in how people live and what defines their culture and experience – EBC mirrored and explored many of these traits and qualities in the lives of her fictional characters, and how those characters countered the powers and obstacles that would prevent their achievement of them.

Moreover, she certainly would have agreed with her writer friend and Sumter County neighbor James McBride Dabbs on his theory of "manners into morals," whereby the traditional Southern emphasis on manners – the ways and gestures by which we show each other courtesy and respect – is actually an expression of morality. Dabbs believed this part of the culture of the Old South was worth recognizing, cultivating and practicing. EBC would have seen the beauty, and the love, in that.

• • • • •

Another dimension of this stylish, elegant woman was her appreciation for the beauty of the earth. If she was a lady who cultivated a refined indoor aesthetic, she was also a woman who loved the out-of-doors. In a blurb on the back of her 1977 book, *Blood Red Roses*, she is identified not only as the author of several novels, but also as "an enthusiastic gardener, teacher, historian and sportswoman." EBC didn't mind getting her hands dirty – growing flowers and vegetables, tending horses and dogs, feeding and watching birds, and hunting wild game. All of these were lifelong passions.

As a Boatwright and a Coker, she cherished the landscape around her native Darlington and Hartsville, with its fertile fields and forests, its meandering rivers and streams. She relished traveling over to historic Edgefield and the peach-growing region around Ridge Spring, in Saluda County, to conduct research or to visit her Boatwright and Watson kinfolk who lived there. No doubt she would have been smitten by the beauty of that gorgeous territory in the springtime when the peach trees were in blossom. And she would have loved getting down to the wondrous sea islands and estuaries of the coast, with its urban anchors of Myrtle Beach, Georgetown, Charleston and Beaufort. Then there was the glory of the mountains at the Coker aerie in Blowing Rock, North Carolina (she was once referred to as an "Adopted Tar Heel Writer"). EBC embraced the Carolinas from the mountains to the sea and knew the region intimately.

• • • • •

Mention of EBC'S attachment to the land, to place, to particular locales, leads to the recognition of an additional love: travel. Travel fed her immense curiosity and provided an avenue for expressing it. Her diaries and novels are replete with detailed accounts of the many places she visited, both in the Americas and the wider world – the cities and towns, the cultures, the geographies, the fauna and flora. Her rich descriptions are a hallmark of her talent as a writer and provide some of the most riveting pieces in this volume. Such passages are essential reading, partly for the way in which they vary in content, mood and tone.

As recounted by Penelope and Eliza, one of EBC's first adventures far from home occurred in New York City in 1929, when as a young college graduate she sought employment as a writer with *The New York Times,* but wound up working briefly as a model. Her short stay gave her a sense of urban energy and excitement – a taste of the flapper life of the Roaring Twenties and the world of F. Scott Fitzgerald's *The Great Gatsby.* It would also change her destiny, for it was in New York she met her future husband, Jim Coker.

Thirty-two years later, the city would take on another, ominous significance for Elizabeth, due to Jim's death there in 1961. Her chronicle of his final days and hours constitutes a particularly gripping example of epistolary writing. It is a deeply touching record of human life-and-death communication – the powerful stuff from which novels are made.

Multiple trips outside the United States followed Jim's death. EBC especially loved visiting Mexico, where she spent a month each year as she got older. Her immersion in Mexican history and culture resulted in the 1981 publication of *The Grasshopper King.* Readers of *A Curious Heart* will want to be sure to find the chapter that focuses on EBC's time in the Yucatan and how she transformed what she learned there into fiction.

And then there is Turkey.

A travel vignette that EBC wrote about a 1964 trip to Istanbul in the company of her brother deserves special attention and comment. Except for the fact that this gathering had to do with a family event, it is totally different in substance, tone and mood from the dark realism and intensity of her requiem for Jim. The inclusion of these two passages in *A Curious Heart* provides convincing evidence of the wide range of EBC's talent and expertise – even when she's writing for an audience of one, namely herself.

Notably, the verbal tableau that EBC creates for her interlude in Istanbul has the redolence of viewing a classical genre painting. One can imagine the blinding Turkish light and color, and see the perfectly rendered human figures against the exotic Middle Eastern backdrop. Some kind of serious, then lighthearted transaction is taking place, with just enough pure darkness and drama to convey a feeling of gravity and tension. An overriding element of uncertainty is present in EBC's depiction, demanding the relief of a positive outcome, which she provides.

EBC has taken a modest travel episode and shaped it into a short story, utilizing the literary conventions of place and time and circumstance (the plot line), along with characterization, dialogue, and a sprinkling of secrecy, suspense and surprise. But most important is the story's theme of family life, and its exploration of love – in a brief voluptuous travel setting within a small knot of kinfolk, with its inherent complications and misunderstandings, revelations and joys.

• • • • •

In his introduction to *South Carolina Literature*, published in 1931 by Hartsville educator John C. Hungerpiller, cultural journalist Stanhope Sams claimed that South Carolina's writers had created something vital and spirited, "a shining achievement." Sams went on to assert that there was "no better or pleasanter way to learn the history, character and quality of a people than through its literature."

This was two decades before EBC's first novel, *Daughter of Strangers*, exploded onto the literary scene. The next four decades would see her become established as a serious, but popular literary and cultural presence in South Carolina and beyond. To use his terms, Stanhope Sams would indeed have certified EBC's novels as "a shining achievement," her work as "vital and spirited." Her writing would be precisely what Sams meant when he emphasized literature as the best and most pleasant way to learn the history, character and quality of a people.

In the volume before you, Penelope and Eliza submit that Elizabeth's writing "provided the portal through which she could wholly embrace and illuminate life – getting to the heart of the human condition in all its joy and sorrow and beauty." They go on to posit that "her love for and faith in writing, where the self and the soul could find full expression, was her polestar." This is what EBC's writing does for her readers. It provides a portal for embracing and illuminating life, a polestar enabling full expression of self and soul.

"I have a feeling heart," EBC once confided to an audience. It is an addendum to her "curious and secret heart." Read on to discover the delightful reality of these thoughts and feelings. Listen to the voice of Elizabeth Boatwright Coker as she reveals herself in her life and letters. Then identify, celebrate and find joy in your own. EBC would have loved your doing so, and would have been curious about what you found, and what you made of it.

– Thomas L. Johnson

[*The lasting friendship between Elizabeth Boatwright Coker and Tom Johnson began during the final 20 years of Elizabeth's life. As a faculty member on staff with the University of South Carolina's South Caroliniana Library, Johnson was instrumental in securing the author's letters and papers for permanent preservation at the Caroliniana Library, where EBC had spent countless hours conducting research. EBC and Johnson served together on the board of governors of the South Carolina Academy of Authors, and Johnson introduced EBC at her induction ceremony into the Academy in 1991. She was a primary source of encouragement to Johnson in his own prize-winning efforts as a poet, editor and writer of short fiction. They shared many literary interests over the decades, and Johnson has written about EBC's life and work on numerous occasions.*]

PREFACE

Nearly a decade ago, we resolved to write a book about our mother and grandmother, Elizabeth Boatwright Coker – a tireless researcher and award-winning author of nine novels, including more than one *New York Times* bestseller. She was also the wife of James Lide Coker III – president of Sonoco Products Company, the world's largest producer of composite cans, tubes and cores for wound products such as paper and textiles. While Elizabeth harnessed her wealth and standing to live the life she wanted, she also defied convention, with one foot in the Old South and the other in the new. She was a woman to be reckoned with: smart, beautiful and bold.

Born in 1909, Elizabeth was the product of a post-Reconstruction South. Segregation was at its zenith and her birthplace of Darlington, South Carolina was no exception. Civil War veterans and formerly enslaved African Americans populated the landscape. A Confederate veterans monument occupied the town's courthouse square.

In 1950, when her first novel, *Daughter of Strangers*, burst on the scene – a daring exploration of racial identity set in antebellum New Orleans and the Carolina Lowcountry – Elizabeth aimed an observant and critical lens on her homeland. While she never foreswore her Southern heritage, she refused to surrender blindly to it.

As we set out to research her story we began to grasp the arc of Elizabeth's full and remarkable life. She was a compulsive writer from a young age and left us copious letters and diaries. Upon exploring her archived papers at the University of South Carolina's South Caroliniana Library, we concluded that Elizabeth herself should do most of the telling.

From the outset, friend and author Tom Johnson – retired English professor and librarian at the University of South Carolina – championed our book and urged us on. We are deeply indebted to Tom, in particular for his beautiful Foreword. We are also grateful to Henry Fulmer, former director of the South Caroliniana Library and Graham Duncan, former collections manager and curator of manuscripts. Graham patiently guided us through the archive and responded quickly and efficiently to our request for a digital copy of Elizabeth's voluminous personal correspondence. Moreover, Nathan Saunders, current director of the South Caroliniana Library, and building manager Rob Smith, generously assisted us with locating and selecting images for the book.

We spent many months reading and familiarizing ourselves with Elizabeth's papers, aided by researcher and writer Jesse Bustos-Nelson and editor and author Virginia Christian Beach. We are truly indebted to Virginia and her involvement in the project that took us to the the finish line with her expertise in book writing and enthusiasm for the subject. Throughout *A Curious Heart*, we have carefully selected and arranged excerpts of Elizabeth's writings. In some instances, readers will note unconventional spellings and punctuation, along with Elizabeth's distinctive dialect – elements we have retained in order to remain true to her story.

One of many revelations during our explorations of the archive was the fact that Converse College provided a turning point for Elizabeth. She was mentored by several influential teachers and writers. As a senior in 1929, she declared: "All my life I have wanted to write a book." But it would be another twenty years before Elizabeth realized her dream. During that time, she marshaled her diverse talents to support her husband, cultivate her community and care for her family. She was "doing what was indicated," as she liked to say, and used her leftover time and energy to become a "closet" writer.

Our "Ma," Elizabeth, was imaginative, generous and fun; and you learned that if you caught her at the right time, she would promise the rainbow. But if you expected the rainbow to arrive and promises to be kept to the letter, you asked "Da." Celebrated in her home state, a spotlight seemed to follow wherever she went. Even the car she drove – a canary yellow Corvette – became the stuff of legend.

Elizabeth had the brains and audacity to do exactly as she pleased. There was never a doubt in her mind. Granted, there were setbacks – an auto accident, cancer, death in the family, rejection by publishers, and so on – but if she ever second-guessed her talents and aspirations, we never knew.

Elizabeth's motto was to "bloom where you are planted." She felt entirely at home wherever she landed and lent a touch of magic to the Coker house on Home Avenue in Hartsville, South Carolina. To her grandchildren visiting from up north, the beds always felt softer, the meals tasted better, and the flurry of activity sparkled brighter in Ma's orb. Best of all, we felt valued and adored in her company.

What's more, Elizabeth was brave, especially during her husband's terrible illness and in later life, growing old alone in a big house. She remained genuinely interested in everything and everyone, and her sense of fun kept her household and friendships lively. The Christmas trees were as big as ever and eggs were hidden every Easter in the garden, even if the youngest finders were now college seniors. Elizabeth never retreated from people and projects, and never stopped writing.

First and foremost, Elizabeth Boatwright Coker's legacy is as a writer, so it is fitting we introduce our protagonist in her own words, excerpted from a 1964 letter to friend and author Ann Head. Recently widowed and at the height of her career, Elizabeth describes the flood of memories as she cleans out the attic of the family home in Hartsville:

> The first day up there I was a child playing ball in the Savannah streets and crabbing in the River May at Bluffton; a flapper waltzing in strong hot arms, [Gus] Wedemeyer and Jan Garber's bands playing "Come to Me, Oh Come My Darling" – laughing, windblown in the rumble seat of a fast, new-style Chrysler convertible, while the moonlit mountains of Saluda and Hendersonville floated by on a wave of summer flirtations; a starry-eyed bride; a loving young mother; a gay sophisticate sipping champagne at the Ritz bar in Paris, being tailored in London, climbing a mountain in Switzerland, winning at craps in the casino at Monte Carlo, meeting fascinating new kinds of people on shipboard and in deluxe hotels, sailing the summer seas on social sailboats. Then again, a mother – not so young a one; a dedicated nurse's aide during World War II; suddenly a successful author; a busy matron – pouring tea, active on boards and committees, healthily galloping my big hunter on the trails at Blowing Rock and through Kellytown; overnight, dramatically facing the years of [husband] Jim's terrible illness and adjustments, [and ultimately] his death. Exciting the battle with the Vanquisher, Jim and I thinking we had a chance to win. Dramatic. Tragic.

A decade after penning this letter, Elizabeth finds herself in another quiet, evocative space – the Franklin Delano Roosevelt Presidential Library in Hyde Park, New York, where she is researching a new book. Much like the attic setting in Hartsville, the venerable archive echoes the past and sparks the author's imagination – unlocking a trove of remembrances and untold tales.

From the FDR Library, we begin Chapter One of the story of our mother and grandmother. She leads us back and forth through a life that spans nearly the entire 20th century. The course of her 84 years is well documented and we recreate key scenes and conversations along the way – based on her letters and diaries, as well as our own remembrances.

But first, we give you a brief Prologue, a snapshot into Elizabeth's world as a young corporate wife. It's December of 1949, on one of many days when she is juggling her hostess duties with her determination to be a novelist. Since childhood, Elizabeth has been tethered to tradition and "what is expected." Yet she is hell bent on moving forward. It is this journey of self-discovery that we wish to share. To paraphrase author and historian Harlan Greene – from a lecture he delivered at the University of South Carolina – she must pay the boatman with a tribute to the past, before she is allowed to cross to another shore.

– The Authors

PROLOGUE

Elizabeth paused at her typewriter for a moment to review plans for the midday meal. Dinner. Not lunch. Lunch was had at the Woman's Exchange in New York. Or the Boyd-Powe drugstore in downtown Hartsville.

Jim and the men from the Manchester, Canada plant would soon be leaving the mill. They were to arrive at 1pm sharp. The man from Mexico would come with Jim's brother, Charles. Mozelle had been persuaded to come back to work for a day to oversee everything; in particular, to fry her own special chicken and make sure the rice and gravy and lady peas and okra and tomatoes and biscuits and chess pie turned out better than just good. And to see that James served properly. He had never been out of the yard before.

The table was set with the finest. Well, the second finest. Nobody would notice anyway. But they would if the chicken was greasy or the napkins wrinkled or if James spilled gravy on their sleeve.

She had a half-hour before her "President's Lady" lunch performance. Leaning on her elbows, she smoothed the paper in the rollers. Why was it so hard to type these last sentences? After all, this was the third complete draft. Come on, Liza – you've thought of the ending a thousand times, written it a hundred. Here goes:

> "Conscious of something beyond their understanding they trooped meekly into the dining room to tell Lula all about it."

Meekly? Why were they meek? Well, really, they just were. It had all been figured out months ago. Leave it. She continued:

> " 'Let's go upstairs until our suppertime,' Leon embraced Charlotte tenderly. And smiling a strange secret smile, she picked up the crab claw and the necklace and hurriedly dropped them back into her reticule together."

These were the final sentences of *Daughter of Strangers*, Elizabeth's inaugural novel, which catapulted to *The New York Times* bestseller list in 1950 and stayed there for months.

Elizabeth hoped she had picked the right name for Charlotte. She had always wished her own name were Charlotte. She meant it to convey beauty and tenderness, strength and strangeness, and determination, all at the same time. She knew how important characters' names were. For heaven's sake, Scarlett's original name had been Pansy. Margaret Mitchell had told her so at the writers' conference in Blowing Rock when Charlotte was only part of a half-written amateur short story. Years later, the wonderful agent – Civil War novelist Clifford Dowdey's literary agent – had told her this: "Nobody wants to read about a spitfire named Pansy. The book would have sunk like a stone . . . But Scarlett . . ."

The End. Finis. Her book was complete. A long time coming. And best of all, *Daughter of Strangers* was going to be read day after tomorrow by the great Elliott Macrae in New York City. She would deliver the manuscript in person, while Jim waited at the St. Regis. She would wear a brand new Babylonian Blue hat from Montaldo's in Charlotte. Yes, the Queen City. Queen Charlotte.

The men were coming in the front door laughing. She walked down the stairs as queenlike as she could.

"Hello gentlemen. Welcome!"

Chapter 1

OTHER SHORES

Elizabeth Boatwright Coker mixed well with the residents of Millbrook, New York. She visited frequently after her daughter, Penelope, married Mortimer Hall – known as Morti by his friends – in 1972. Morti was the former treasurer of *The New York Post*. His mother, Dorothy Schiff, was the famously hands-on owner and publisher of the popular left-leaning newspaper.

The Halls had moved into a large house on a rundown former dairy farm. Their blended family included Morti and Penelope, six horses, four dogs, Penelope's small daughter Eliza, and four of Morti's five children – three little girls and a boy. Their mother, the actress Diana Lynn, had died the year before. There was also a "tight English nanny" and a temporary barn fixer and horse keeper, borrowed from Morti's uncle, John Schiff.

The family undertook a renovation of the 18th century farmhouse, which Elizabeth described as "still in the process of becoming modern . . . one rambles through ten bedrooms and endless crooked halls and chintzy living rooms and shiny kitchens till one grows dizzy, wondering which is your stair and which *your* little gabled hideaway."

The new occupants named their home "The Hall of Halls" and were soon presenting it and themselves to Millbrook locals, fox hunters, horse people in nearby Hyde Park and Pawling, friends in New York and from Penelope's previous life in Ridgefield, Connecticut. Before long, the Hall family (and The Hall of Halls) became a fixture of what passed for Millbrook society. Dolly Schiff and Elizabeth met for the first time at Christmas and tested each other's mettle, as mothers-in-law will.

When first introduced, Mrs. Schiff thought it would be fun to shock a "Southern country bunny," remembered Elizabeth. She opened with a question: "Darling, do you have a lover?" Without missing a beat, Elizabeth responded: "Of course! Don't you? I may not always have shoes, but I *always* have a lover." Each had met her match and knew it.

• • • • •

Elizabeth had been traveling with a vengeance since her husband Jim's death from cancer in 1961 – as much to avoid being home alone in Hartsville or at their mountain house in Blowing Rock, as to be distracted by new places. Eventually, Millbrook would instill affection and pride of place, largely because of her daughter and granddaughter.

At the time, social life in Millbrook was dominated by equestrian endeavors, especially the hunt and everything associated with it: hounds, hunt breakfasts, hunt balls, horse shows, etc. Franklin D. Roosevelt, Jr., one of the town's more illustrious residents, preferred it to Hyde Park, the Roosevelt family seat. He found Millbrook a pleasant refuge from politics, business ventures and his many wives and would-be wives. He was a neighbor of the Halls and long-time friend of Morti.

When Elizabeth and Franklin, Jr. met, they had an instant rapport, undoubtedly due to their shared love of horses. He was master of the neighboring hunt and an avid carriage driver. Elizabeth was a proficient horsewoman. She and the Halls became frequent guests at the Roosevelt estate on Campobello Island. Franklin, Jr., was eager to have a book written about his grandmother Sara Delano Roosevelt. Elizabeth – a new friend and accomplished author – became his choice of biographer.

Coincidentally, Elizabeth was spending lengthy periods of time at the FDR Presidential Library in Hyde Park in hopes of resurrecting a book project she had started decades earlier. The library was located close to Millbrook and provided the author a quiet and convenient retreat for research and writing.

• • • • •

Fast forward to the 1980s and Elizabeth is back in Millbrook, spending a few weeks with Penelope and Eliza while Morti is on his boat and the Hall children are off at boarding school. It is a blustery day and Penelope steers the family station wagon up the drive to the entrance of the house, just as her mother pops out the front door.

"Ah," Penelope says, "no pencil skirt today." Her mother sports a lavender cropped jacket and matching plaid A-line skirt, with black flats, black turtleneck and one of her most becoming cold-weather hats – a large, soft felt – tilted just so. Elizabeth opens the front passenger door and sits down erect and smiling.

"You're looking rather sensible today," quips Penelope. "Another day at the mill with the librarians?"

Elizabeth smiles enigmatically, "Oh yes, another day at the mill."

Penelope nods and lets her gaze linger on the large, soft *chapeau*. "That's a rather formidable hat . . . Are you expecting more snow and a freeze before I bring you home this afternoon?"

"No dear, it's the library – colder than usual last week," responds Elizabeth. "The librarians and the Roosevelts like it that way. Helps preserve all that paper."

"It's a Groton thing, Ma; all the Roosevelt men go there . . . It's those cold-water showers and shivery classrooms. It was warmer in girls' boarding schools. Six years of Groton and a man will get used to the cold," Penelope declares and pulls out on the road in the direction of Hyde Park.

Both women laugh as they roar off. Within 20 minutes they arrive at the parking lot of the large stone, Dutch colonial edifice of the FDR Presidential Library and Museum. Once through the entrance, Elizabeth greets the desk staff, signs in and withdraws pencils and a steno pad before stashing her pocketbook in a locker.

Claiming her customary chair at a heavy, wooden table in the corner of the main reading room, she requests a cache of archival papers from the reference librarian. The young woman rolls out a metal book cart full of folders and doles them out one at a time for Elizabeth to examine. Pausing only occasionally to look out the window, Elizabeth methodically works her way through the documents.

By late morning she is ahead of schedule and it's time for a break. Elizabeth decides to brave the cold and take a short walk outside around the back of the library to where FDR and Eleanor are buried. Speculating briefly about the relationship between the late president and first lady, she then shakes her head and mutters the old English admonition: "Away with the fairies! Get back to reality, Elizabeth."

Back inside Elizabeth dives into another stack of documents, but her mind continues to wander. Her eyes lift from the table and fix on an old oak tree visible through the window, its thick limbs bare and silvery against the winter sky. The ancient tree seems to conjure time passing, while at the same time bringing it to a standstill. Her thoughts drift south, back to her youth in Darlington, to a warm, green world full of light and shadow. There, the oaks hold onto their leaves through the winter, waiting until spring to shed old growth making way for new – hence the name "live" oak. Spanish moss drapes the live oaks' horizontal limbs like funeral shrouds, punctuated by green ribbons of resurrection fern unfurling along the branches.

Through the haze of memory, Elizabeth recalls a happy childhood – thanks not so much to her mother as to her beloved father and brothers. The pace of life is gentle and slow in Darlington. Children roam freely. Relations of one kind or another are around every corner. At the same time, ghosts from the past come out of nowhere, seeping into everything like mold and mildew. Growing up in small-town South Carolina is both a blessing and a burden.

Chapter 2

CHILDHOOD MUSES

Long before Darlington became indelibly associated with the roar of the racetrack – stock car, that is – it was known as a modest cotton town, with a relaxed but busy social life. Born on April 21, 1909 to Purvis Jenkins Boatwright, an elegant planter-banker, and Bessie Hurd Boatwright, a redhead with a wicked sense of humor, Elizabeth joined two older brothers named William (age 7) and James (age 5).

Elizabeth always felt she arrived in a world bathed in the glimmering twilight of the Old South, when life seemed sweet, simple and brimming with possibility. Unlike most small towns, Darlington's tight-knit community had an appetite for culture and innovation. The local opera house hosted travelling companies en route to Charleston or Columbia, ranging in attractions from the Metropolitan Opera to the African American-owned traveling show, Silas Green from New Orleans. As a child, Elizabeth thrilled to a live production of "Ben Hur," with real chariot races staged around the town square.

> [Town square] was where we came together to share sorrow or to give thanks for our deliverance and high happenings; or just to catch hands and point toes in celebration of whatever was indicated.

Horse shows, fire engine races, political speakers, square dances and fireworks were all held on the live oak-lined courthouse square. One of Elizabeth's earliest memories was walking downtown at dusk, hand in hand with her handsome father to await the results of the 1913 presidential election. She watched Purvis Boatwright throw his wide-brimmed Panama hat in the air, giving three undignified cheers as the winner's name was written on a board in front of the courthouse steps: that of one-time South Carolina resident Woodrow Wilson.

• • • • •

Summers were spent with Elizabeth's favorite aunts – Reitta and Ethel Boatwright, sisters of her father – either at Ridge Spring, the family cotton plantation near Edgefield, or at Shady Branch (owned by Ethel and her husband, Lockwood Clancy) on the May River near Hilton Head. "They had a relaxed, easy way of life," Elizabeth later told a *Charlotte Observer* reporter, "and held to some of the ways of the Old South. But they still looked to the New South. They read the daily *New York Times* there in that remote area, *Harper's* magazine and the *Yale Review*, [which] was my Aunt Ethel's favorite."

They also taught their niece how to cook and tell tall tales. Elizabeth would model her home life on theirs.

> At Shady Branch, my aunts, uncles, cousins, brothers and I would sit on the long front piazza in the warm dark. Each was required to tell one story of something interesting or awful that happened during the day. If you reneged or told a boring story, you were drummed to the outer darkness over to the joggling board under the big holly tree, beyond listening distance, for ten miserable minutes.

If Reitta and Ethel were her muses, Elizabeth's older brothers were her heroes. William and James brought intrigue and adventure to her childhood. Games like Pop the Whip, Red Rover and Kick the Can filled their summer days. The twilight hours inspired a cast of imaginary characters engaged in fantastical capers.

Elizabeth had a flair for the dramatic and soon gained a reputation for confident femininity paired with strength and determination – all of which she attributed to her birth sign: Taurus rising under Venus' rule. "I could have been content with social and intellectual success within the close Southern society into which I was born," remarked Elizabeth in her journal. "This, however, was not possible because of my intense physical energy and a feverish ambition and stubborn refusal to accept second-best or half-truths."

• • • • •

Elizabeth was her father's favorite. Purvis was a natural marksman and loved the outdoors, and the added pleasure of getting away from the daily challenges of work and family. Elizabeth noticed how he became a different person in the wild. "The fact is, I had a god when I was a child, and that god was in the image of Daddy."

She cemented their bond by becoming a skilled shooter. Much to Purvis' delight, Elizabeth stayed a good shot throughout her life – whether killing venomous snakes in the woods near their home, or on bird shooting expeditions in distant lands. Describing her first experiences with a gun, she observed, "I cried inside whenever the quail or dove or ducks came spiraling down in a spray of feathers; never, apparently, causing my hand to tremble or my eyes to waver. The two words, death and hit, did not seem synonymous."

Elizabeth remembered hunting with her father on winter afternoons as some of the happiest experiences of her childhood: "In the woods, Mama wasn't around with her over-sentimentality or outrageously funny, yet cruel wit. She could be left to lounge lazily on a wicker *chaise* reading the classics or a naughty French novel while pans scorched and pots boiled over, as if the cook had the evening off."

Brother James was also a good shot. Once at the county fair, he won a shooting clay contest and bestowed the prize of a fat celluloid doll on his sister.

> I called [the doll] Mike and insisted my nurse, Maum Betsy, bathe him along with me in the tin tub before the nursery fireplace. Somehow in the process of bathing and warming by the fire, Mike's outer layer of face peeled off – to my howl of horror – and he disappeared into the voluminous folds of Maum Betsy's cambric apron.
>
> Mama had once told James that Maum Betsy used to be a slave and had once birthed a little boy baby. One night she rolled on top of [the baby] in her sleep and smothered him to death. Her master had beaten her for destroying his property.
>
> Our grandfather had bought her and made her our father's "dah." Standing on top of my brother's shoulders, I peeped through Maum Betsy's window one night. She was smoking a pipe by the little fire, holding the doll in her lap.

> "Now, Sugar," she was saying, "Yo daddy coming soon, rat down the chimbly. He make himsely out of smoke, and speak to me." [Suddenly] my foot slipped and we all tumbled down, making a ruckus. We ran like crazy and found our way into a nearby cemetery. To us, the ghosts in the fallen dark were less frightening than the one forming from [the] smoke behind us in the cabin.

• • • • •

Years later, this incident became the subject of a 1926 story Elizabeth submitted to a literary publication while a student at Converse College. Like author DuBose Heyward, who used a similar story his mother told about an enslaved girl and her wooden doll named Porgo (genesis of his novel *Porgy*), Elizabeth was mining a rich reservoir of oral tradition. But the tale of Maum Betsy and her baby proved too shocking to print. Nevertheless, Elizabeth's English professor praised it and encouraged her to keep writing. Elizabeth identified this story as the germ of her first novel, *Daughter of Strangers*.

Even as a little girl during the First World War, Elizabeth was compelled to put words on paper. She began by composing poetry.

> The Brown thrush keeps singing, "A nest do you see
> And five eggs hid by me in the juniper tree?"
> Don't meddle! Don't touch! Little girl, little boy,
> or the world will lose some of its joy
> "Now I'm glad! Now I'm free
> And I always shall be,
> If you never bring sorrow for me."

Meanwhile, unbeknownst to the budding young writer, Baltimore native and critic H. L. Mencken was igniting a firestorm with his infamous essay, "The Sahara of the Bozart." Published in 1917 in the *New York Evening Mail*, the diatribe charged that the South was "almost as sterile, intellectually, artistically, culturally, as the Sahara Desert." Mencken described most Southern poetry and prose as "drivel."

Among other criticisms, he lambasted the Southern institution of white men's mulatto mistresses. Miscegenation was becoming a fascination of American cultural entertainment, as exemplified by D.W. Griffith's hugely popular film "Birth of a Nation," released in 1915, and Jerome Kern's and Oscar Hammerstein's 1927 Broadway hit musical "Show Boat." A quarter-century later, Elizabeth would make miscegenation the central theme of her breakout novel.

• • • • •

Elizabeth's first writing project to deliver tangible results was "Noches," a tender bit of verse about two *vaqueros* riding across a desert to the soft, silvery sound of jangling spurs. The poem won the 1925 Poetry Society of South Carolina's Ellen M. Carroll Prize. It was the result of Elizabeth's being punished for daydreaming in Latin class at St. John's High School. The young poet received $25 and a congratulatory letter from Poetry Society president John Bennett. "I was hooked," she would say later. "Money having been earned, I had become a writer."

Elizabeth credited Susie Brunson, principal of St. John's from 1905 to 1946, for inspiring her to aim high. "She took a special interest in me and encouraged me," recounted Elizabeth. "She was the one who sent my poems to the Charleston Poetry Society and other places where I won awards. She was just as proud of me as if I were her own daughter."

Elizabeth was an avid diary keeper as a teenager and recorded her growing interest in the opposite sex. There were always numerous invitations, dates to parties, joy rides and dances. In her entry for November 18, 1923, she wrote:

> Well I can safely say that this was my first experience of "puppy love" as grownups would say; yet when one is fifteen, a good-looking boy that can play football, who has brown waving hair, wonderful eyes and a grand mouth and at whose touch, little prickles run over you and he shows that he likes you a little, well one can't be blamed.

At age 16, a car crash dealt Elizabeth a near mortal blow when Purvis picked her up from school one afternoon. She and her father escaped life threatening injuries, but the accident left Elizabeth with a broken collarbone, broken jaw and several lost teeth. During her months-long recovery, she felt forlorn, disfigured and isolated . . . desperate that her lovely face would never be the same. Her mother's comment of "Now she'll never get a husband" stung her mightily.

Her father refused to let her wallow in self-pity. He drove her through town in their red Overland touring car, forcing Elizabeth to smile, wave and speak pleasantly to everyone they encountered. "This was a hard thing to do; but harder was learning to greet each day, as well as to meet each day. To realize that the world was not a cushion to be sat on, but a challenge that must be met."

Ultimately, the episode strengthened her ability to accept disappointment and loss. She learned the necessity of moving beyond self-absorption, obliging her to become more engaging and generous with others.

Humor also served Elizabeth well, as she later told Edward R. Murrow on his nationally syndicated radio show, "This I Believe." "I believe in the blessed balm of laughter," she said. "Even laughing in the dark is a more melodious sound to our Creator than whimpering over fears and incapacities . . . If we place the proper value on laughter, we learn to believe in tolerance, which, in the end, is my strongest credo."

Chapter 3

BECOMING A WRITER

In the autumn of 1925, Elizabeth joined the freshman class at Converse College, an all girls' institution founded in 1889 in Spartanburg, South Carolina. She was the first female in her family to pursue higher education and threw herself into her studies. Women had won the right to vote just five years prior.

Converse transformed Elizabeth – expanding her views of the world and deepening her desire to become a writer. But it was not all work and no play. There were Christmas balls at Clemson, June hops at The Citadel, fraternity parties at Carolina, dances at Davidson, house parties at the beach, and lakeside gatherings in the mountains.

Elizabeth's reputation as a talented poet preceded her. She was enlisted as part of freshman "hazing" to write three poems for the school literary publication, *The Concept*. All of her poems were accepted. Named the class poet, she contributed regularly to the magazine. By her junior year, she was its editor. Under her leadership, the South Carolina College Press Association voted *The Concept* the best college magazine in the state.

With encouragement from her professors, Elizabeth received more and more accolades for her writing, with works published in *Harper's Magazine* and *The Saturday Evening Post*. In 1928, she won the coveted Poetry Society of South Carolina's John Bennett Skylark Prize for a work entitled "Red Moon:"

> There will be a red moon some night.
> Some night when the world is a fairy ring,
> Clouded with gossamer light.
> And the wee man that dusts off the track,
> Will be fast asleep on a honey bee's back.
> Then the moon will come over a lone fir tree.
> Over the fir tree with a crimson smile,
> And the moon will beckon to me.
> So I will hurry and catch the moon,
> E'r she climbs from the lone fir tree,

> And over the hills and dreamy lagoons,
> We will go to the Tankor's sea.
>
> Laugh if you will – but remember,
> There will be a red moon some night!

The prize was named for author John Bennett, a founding member in 1920 of The Poetry Society of South Carolina – America's oldest state poetry society. Other founders included DuBose Heyward and Josephine Pinckney. Bennett was one of the few nonnatives. He hailed from Ohio, but after arriving in Charleston, married into the prominent Smythe family. As an outsider, he had less of a vested interest in South Carolina's Confederate past than his Southern friends. He also recognized African Americans' enormous contribution to the national culture and elevated them in his novels, endowing his Black characters with dignity and agency.

Another author to do so was South Carolina native Julia Peterkin. All of Peterkin's novels featured African Americans whom she had come to know while living on her husband's inland cotton plantation near Forte Motte. Historian Harlan Greene describes Peterkin's storytelling: "Her Black characters leapt off the page. She made them real. How dare a white woman write of such things?"

Peterkin graduated from Converse College in 1896 at the age of 16 and went on to earn a master's degree there. Some three decades later, in 1929, she won the Pulitzer Prize for her novel *Scarlet Sister Mary*. Peterkin was the first Southern author to win the Pulitzer for fiction. That same year, she returned to her alma mater to speak. Elizabeth, as editor of Converse's literary magazine, was invited to interview the bestselling writer. At first the college senior was star-struck; but soon the encounter led to mentorship, and eventual friendship, between author and student. In a commencement address at Coker College years later, Elizabeth recounted that first meeting:

> Julia Peterkin's image at the time was composed of sharp, twinkling eyes in an almost masculine, freckled face, framed by a glory of red hair. She described herself as "the most beautiful ugly woman in the world." Her tall gaunt frame carried about it an ineffable elegance and presence. In a deep rich voice, she

> told about her consciousness of living on a South Carolina plantation far away from the literary center of things; the loneliness of being a writer; the thrill of it. A natural raconteur, she let us in on amusing secrets about herself, her family, her characters. I adored her.

The two kept in touch and exchanged letters. After the publication of *Daughter of Strangers* in 1950, Peterkin came out of seclusion to attend Elizabeth's first public speaking engagement at the University of South Carolina.

In a subsequent commencement speech Elizabeth gave, she recognized the mentors and teachers at Converse who had shaped her college experience and motivated her to become a writer. "In my sophomore year, there was a flame-haired, wildly dramatic Miss Helen Smith. Witty, often sarcastically so, and full of exaggerations, she encouraged my tendency to view simple happenings as high romance; and to think things through in terms of exciting denouement and pure story."

Reflecting on other factors that fueled her passion for literature, she stated, "I began story writing as soon as I learned what words were made of. I have always been a gluttonous reader. I think writers of imaginative narrative stories based on believable human beings have probably been my greatest influences, such as Tolstoy, Balzac, Flaubert, Sigrid Undset, the Brontë [sisters], etc."

As graduation approached in the spring of 1929, Elizabeth resolved to move to New York City and pursue her dream of becoming a writer. She was 20 years old.

Chapter 4

NEW YORK CITY

Every now and again I have suddenly had the illusion that youth has not vanished entirely . . . . What heaven to be twenty again! Just for a little moment in time.

– Elizabeth Boatwright Coker

Elizabeth could seize only "a little moment" of big city life. Within six months of graduation from Converse, the Roaring Twenties came to a halt and Elizabeth found herself at the epicenter of the financial collapse. She soon bade goodbye to New York City, but not before taking in much of its glamour and glitz.

In June of 1929, Elizabeth and her like-minded classmate, Mary Shipp, boarded the New York-bound Atlantic Coast Line Railroad at the McBee depot – a tiny brick station in McBee, South Carolina, 26 miles from Darlington. Elizabeth had collected enough graduation money from various relatives to pay for a train ticket and a few months' rent. Mary, her partner in adventure, also wanted to be a writer.

The two friends began their new lives at The Parnassus Club, a "bastion of respectability" on West 115th Street – offering lodging to women enrolled at the Julliard School of Music, Barnard College and Columbia University. Assorted female artists, writers and semiprofessional performers rounded out the residents. Elizabeth and Mary lasted two weeks before moving to more bohemian quarters on West 121st Street. The small, inexpensive room north of the university was their gateway to the dazzle of New York City – a town they both intended to conquer.

"The Land of Ambition and Success," as F. Scott Fitzgerald famously described America's premiere city, was a whole new world to Elizabeth. Imposing skyscrapers like the *Daily News* Building, the Chrysler Building and the Empire State Building had recently risen up on Manhattan Island. More and more people were migrating to the metropolis – whether they be refugees from Eastern Europe and the Jim Crow South, or artists and writers determined to make their mark. Nothing was too high or too far.

Women, in particular, enjoyed more freedom and independence in the mixing bowl that was New York. In particular, the "youth culture" of the 1920s – aka the Jazz Age – allowed for a kind of personal freedom and movement unheard of in small-town South Carolina. The Big Apple epitomized the excitement, the restlessness and the *laissez-faire* attitude of the post-World War I, pre-Great Depression era in America. Elizabeth was all in.

While waiting for jobs to materialize, she and Mary were fortunate to have several beaux in the city – mostly boys from home – to pay for dinners and dancing in the evenings. The girls found they also got hungry during the day, which meant interim jobs to pay for regular, if "Hopperesque," meals at the local automat.

Mary was hired by Dell Publishing to write blurbs for *True Story* magazine and Elizabeth got a job modeling hats and shoes. In those pre-Ford Agency days, a model lived by her wits as well as her walk. As Elizabeth recounted later, she lost her first job after her boss offered her free pairs of silk stockings on condition that he be allowed to put one pair on her legs. She refused. In a letter home, while still modeling shoes, she wrote: "Thin though they may be, my legs are filling up my stomach."

During her six months in New York, Elizabeth dutifully apprised her parents of her activities in letters home to Darlington:

> Dear Momma and Daddy, I crashed Wall Street again today and went from Maiden Lane to Broadway looking for a job, but there aren't any openings except for girls who can use a typewriter. Tell them you have a college diploma and they laugh.
>
> Went to a big-league baseball game yesterday. There were 75,000 people there and I had a box seat. My German took me.
>
> Dick Littlejohn took me to a show the other night and I have a date with Jack Boineau tonight. But he 'cometh not,' as you like to say, Mama.
>
> I am wild about New York. It is intensely interesting and I certainly did need it. (Saturday now) Jack and I went to see

"The Desert Song" last night and then went to the Palais D'Or and danced and then got on the subway and went to Riverside Drive and sat on a bench awhile and watched the lights over the water. We are going to Coney Island on Wednesday. I am resting up today as I am pretty tired of looking for a job.

Oh yes. At the ball game I mentioned, Babe Ruth knocked two home runs – so I have seen something.

Devotedly, E.

Elizabeth kept up a busy social life, with a different date every night – dancing, seeing the sights, making enough money to get along and every so often buy a new pair of shoes. Then one afternoon, James Lide Coker III (a fraternity brother of her brother James from the University of North Carolina) called Elizabeth for a date. She had no time on such short notice, so she proposed a "late date." After an already planned engagement, she suggested they go to Harlem's popular Cotton Club on the corner of 142nd Street and Lenox Avenue. Elizabeth knew of the Coker family, as did her parents. They were considered quite wealthy, even if they were from Hartsville, a small town not far from Darlington.

The date was a success. Jim Coker was shy, but Elizabeth got him talking. He laughed as she described her various jobs. Afterwards, she wrote her parents:

Jim was so sympathetic that I went with him to a tea dance at the Plaza the next afternoon. On Sunday, we rode in one of the carriages in Central Park, and later rode the roller coaster at Coney Island. Jim was frightened. I was thrilled. Jim is a Harvard Business School graduate, and an up-and-coming businessman. His family has a paper spool and tube and container company called Sonoco Products Company.

• • • • •

In 1929, with the closing of banks across America ominously presaging the Great Depression, Elizabeth got word that things were not going well at home. She wrote to her father, who was president of Carolina National Bank in Darlington:

> My Darling Daddy,
>
> Have just heard from Mama concerning the bank failing and I admit it has completely knocked me over. Of course, I won't write any checks – and if there is any way in the world that I can be of the slightest help or use to you, please let me do it. I'm a big girl now and old enough for responsibilities, so please give me the privilege – yes, it would be a privilege to help share yours.
>
> I have a bill for two dresses that is unpaid, but I can wait at least three months for that; otherwise I can get along O.K. Please don't worry over it too much, Daddy. It's only natural that you should care, and it would be inhuman not to. But remember that you have three people (my brothers and me) that are young and strong and willing to do anything that can possibly be of any benefit to you.
>
> Remember that always I love you more completely than anything in all the world.
>
> Your own, Baby

So, it was time to come home to South Carolina. Jim returned to Hartsville and Elizabeth to Darlington. She left a trail of broken hearts in New York. Suitors wrote and pleaded with her to return. She and Jim began dating.

In July 1930, Jim wrote:

> Lib dearest . . . please excuse me for the other night. I was dead tired and worn out mentally. I'm not normally like that, but I haven't been natural for some time, and I can see that I won't be until this uncertainty is over . . . It isn't uncertainty of your love

> that worries me; it isn't jealousy so much. It's uncertainty as to what you will do. Here is all I can suggest. Marry me soon. Very soon. We'll take my money and go to Europe. Before we marry, I will leave Sonoco and get a job anywhere you'd like to live if you don't think we could be happy in Hartsville . . . Sometimes it seems unbearable anyway. A little, ordinary small town with everybody gossiping about your business. It's terrible at times. And yet when I get away, I want to come back; and when I'm here, I want to leave.

Two months later, on September 30, 1930, the young couple married and immediately settled in Hartsville. In taking the leap of faith to forge a new life with Jim, Elizabeth felt conflicted over her dream of being a writer. In a letter from a close family friend she called "Uncle Charlie," it was clear what most people thought she should do.

> Dearest Elizabeth,
>
> So, you are going to take my advice? Only do so if your heart dictates. But remember, there is just as much of a career in the social world as in any of the other walks of life. A woman with your mind should shine as a *chatelaine* and make a man's life something to make him more than proud of you. I know you would have been a success as a writer. You think in your own way and that is about all there is to the literature of our times. I'm sure you would be a success far above average, but there are so many young people writing that the avocation or trade has got a bit commonplace. And what is to hinder an ambitious young woman from doing very brilliant things while she makes a success of her husband . . .
>
> Affectionately, "Uncle" Charlie

But Elizabeth was not interested in what others thought. She decided she would have it both ways.

Chapter 5

HARTSVILLE

After a brief but sparkling interlude in New York, Elizabeth had left one small town in South Carolina only to return to another. Darlington and Hartsville were a bare 15 miles apart, yet there was a definite difference between the two. As she put it, "Darlington was a sleepy, courthouse glamorous town. Hartsville was a busy, mill glamorous town. In Darlington, we ate dinner at two o'clock in the afternoon then rested. In Hartsville, they ate dinner at night . . . [and] ate lunch at 12 o'clock in the day."

Darlington remained a vestige of the Old South, while Hartsville symbolized the new – a company town where mill workers punched a time clock. The haves lived up on the proverbial hill, and everyone else worked down below at the Sonoco plant – a successful packaging business founded by the Cokers which supplied cones, tubes and containers to the textile industry.

Not long out of Harvard Business School, eldest son James, and his younger brother Charles, worked at the plant under their father, Charles Westfield Coker ("Mr. C.W."). It was understood that when Mr. C.W. died, James would become president of the company. No one imagined it would happen any time soon.

Then, in November of 1931, Elizabeth's husband, age 26, was propelled into the role of chief executive after his father died suddenly of a heart attack. They had been married only a year when Jim became president of Sonoco Products Company, a firm begun by his grandfather, Major James Lide Coker. Major Coker was a Confederate veteran and officer, and a leading entrepreneur in the postbellum New South.

In 1889, Major Coker and his son James, Jr., established the first plant to produce wood pulp commercially from Southern pine. Ten years later, "The Major" and his youngest son, Charles (Jim's father), incorporated the Southern Novelty Company, which used pine pulp to manufacture the paper cones and tubes needed in yarn mills across the United States. In 1923 the two enterprises merged to form Sonoco, which grew into a major international producer of yarn carriers and packaging products, eventually becoming a Fortune 500 company and making the Coker family one of the richest in South Carolina.

• • • • •

Jim and Elizabeth's first Hartsville residence was a plain wooden house painted a cheerful yellow. Small but pleasant, it was located not far from the Coker family seat along a dirt road lined with grand trees known as Home Avenue. On March 19, 1932, their first child, Penelope, was born.

Elizabeth adored Jim's father – whom she called "Big Charles" – nearly as much as she adored her own father. The two families spent Sunday nights together enjoying a meal from Mrs. Coker's cook, who, with the evening off, always left food prepared for the family to warm up. Jim's mother (born Carolina "Carrie" Lide of Darlington) worshipped her son and would enlist his help in the kitchen getting supper on the table.

Out in the living room, Elizabeth and Big Charles were forming a strong attachment. He gave her his poetry to peruse and admired her clothes. Big Charles read everything, liked music and loved jokes. Elizabeth sensed her father-in-law was searching for more out of life, much like herself. As she later wrote, "I felt I had a new friend for my new life."

Elizabeth also realized that her husband's diminutive, devoted mother – with her small grey bun, size three shoes and lovely dresses – was as powerful as Jim's father. Thus, the two Mrs. Cokers built a mutually respectful and polite partnership, especially after Big Charles' premature death at the age of 52. Elizabeth described her new life in the following diary entry:

> We built our house, Jim and I, on the property chosen by his father. We dug azaleas and daffodils and wild camellias from the woods, and replanted them on our hill leading up to the house [above] Black Creek. Jim had hired the famous Loutrel Briggs as architect. The rooms he designed were enormous; but how did we ever do with the tiny closets and bathrooms? Briggs was not interested in the mundane. Almost everything I had imagined in college was coming true. But I soon realized how much I had to learn. And how fast we had to grow up. When Jim was elected president of Sonoco in the depths of the Depression (November 1931), there was great demand for the goods Sonoco provided. I put my little writing beginnings away for the moment. We both wanted to succeed together in

our new lives and we worked hard. I had a lot to learn about being what was later called "a company wife." For Sonoco had become an important growing company and the strain on Jim was enormous. He was travelling too much. Working too hard. Drinking too much. I often thought of a poem I had written at Converse:

If I were a lady with an aquiline nose
And with hair of molten gold,
I'd build me a house on yonder hill
With turrets, tall and bold.

And in my house I'd have great chairs
And a vase with a crack in its side,
While a conch shell would be on my mantle
With the sound of the sea at flood tide.

But the heart of my house – the fireplace
With brass andirons, would be,
And when the day had gone to sleep
Firelight would shine on you – and me.

• • • • •

Elizabeth was torn between her enchanted life in Hartsville and the literary life she yearned for. More than anything, she wanted to write a book. Her attempts to reconcile the two are evident in a letter to her friend and New York roommate Mary Shipp (Baker):

I was sorry not to see more of you when you were home and hear a little gossip of 42nd Street and the young S.C. colony.

After our heavenly trip to Bermuda [on honeymoon], where we – the young enchanteds –rode along the path by the sea and laughed at the moon trail and the flame hibiscus and the horse driver and at life.

Then Hartsville and a round of teas and "pleased to meet you's" and ear trumpets – lots of old *fogettes* in black beaded georgette dresses – [and] young wives who wore green velvet hats with brown hose!

That's a partial resume. The present is that there are lots of interesting people here. Miss Taylor – teaching art at Coker College, just back from a year in Italy and a visit to the Duchess Sermoneta who has just written "Things Past." She has given me some quaint Majolica teacups and a modernistic Russian print to go in the living room. She's that sort of person.

There's Cousin Edgar Lawton's wife – Louise Amis from Virginia who studied music with famous teachers and had a studio in Paris.

Dick Coker's mother – back from six months in Africa, who serves afternoon tea and midnight supper.

Oh yes, and me. Between business trips I have just planted some radishes and onions and parsley and am having the preacher to supper tonight!

Harper's has put one of my poems in an anthology of young poets for which Christopher Morley is writing the introduction. I'll send you one when it is published.

Jim is as much a bird of passage as I am. But read this at night and if we're not travelling, we'll be sitting on the divan in front of blazing logs, Jim dreamily smoking and reading things like Bedier's *Tristram* [*and Iseult*].

It's a wonderful life.

Now write me about you. Lib

Decades later, the legendary editor, publisher and author Jonathan Daniels, would introduce Elizabeth at one of her many book events. He read a piece he had written for *The Island Packet* (the South Carolina newspaper he founded on Hilton Head Island) describing those early years when Elizabeth was just beginning to realize her dream:

> Elizabeth and the gentlemen she had found made such a combination of youth and wealth and beauty as Scott Fitzgerald and his Gatsby dreamed about but never found. Aladdin seemed to have arrived first. With them companies of young and fair swam and dived in a private swimming pool in the days before swimming pools became everybody's essential adjuncts in the American way. His [Jim's] mills showed lit windows at night and from the creek below it, their house when illuminated, looked like the diamond as big as the Ritz . . . as for Elizabeth, she keeps wonder wherever she moves. Stardust and daydreams are never long absent from her great big sleepy blue eyes. But be not beguiled. The serpent's tongue can flicker in a smile.

Daniels, described by *The Charlotte Observer* as "a graceful writer and tart social critic . . . a force for progress," had served as press secretary to Franklin D. Roosevelt. He also kept a diary, which resulted in the book *White House Witness 1942-1945: An Intimate Diary of the Years with F.D.R.,* published by Doubleday. Daniels was the first to publicly reveal FDR's affair with Lucy Mercer Rutherford. He and his wife, Lucy Daniels, eventually moved to Hilton Head in 1970. They remained devoted friends of Elizabeth's.

Chapter 6

BLOWING ROCK: HAPPINESS IS A TALL KING

Elizabeth soon realized that her dream of becoming both a successful wife and writer would require more than her own determination. She revealed as much in this passage from her journal, reflecting on the 1930s:

> We were entertaining a lot. At home I hardly had time to do anything else. I realized that I was not only seen as a party person, but as a grownup and that grownups needed help sometimes. As if by magic, my doctor brother James (P.J.) did me an enormous favor. He had operated on a black man who would need a long recovery. The patient worried so about being out of work in these hard times that he asked P.J. if he could help his young wife get a job. She had never worked before. She was handsome, smart, sensible and as bossy as I was. Her name was Mozelle Richardson and she came to me and together we learned how to keep a house. Now I had another friend.
>
> For a while, I kept a portable typewriter in the dressing room; and in fact, between bridge and Cokes in the morning, and meetings with other young wives in the afternoon, and entertaining visiting businessmen in the evenings, I tried to squeeze in the time to write short (very short) stories and poems – like "Sister Mary Magdalene, an offertory in tap time." I don't know where it came from, but it was one of my efforts:
>
> I'm through working hard
> In the cotton fields –
> I'm through hoeing corn
> Till my hands are raw –
> Standing in the swamp till my toes rot off.

Snake in the honeysuckle
Possum in the hollow
Preacher in the pulpit
Shouting sin and sorrow!

I'm through I tell you
Can you hear me down there?
I'm through with croker sacks,
Galling my shoulders.
Glory Hallelujah –
Harlem's finished that!
Now my amber shoulders
Gleam in the arc light.
Folks in the nightclub
Love satin shoulders;
Love golden hips that
Swing like Salome's
My Bubba stay where
Frogs cry all night
Knee deep-jug er rum
Good lord deliver him
Bring him to salvation!

I hear Hi-de-ho!
And my cheeks get hot.
I hear Hi-de-ho and my breath comes fast
Judgment Day is coming!
Gabriel blow your horn!
Louder, yaller trumpeter –
Don't you know I'm Sister
Mary Magdalene –
Tapping out my heart
In my scarlet shoes?

• • • • •

Fifty years later, Elizabeth finds herself once again in Hyde Park, New York – still seated at the FDR Library, daydreaming instead of studying the archives. She pushes away from the oak table in the corner, knees and ankles together. Slanting her legs to the side, she looks down and considers her black flats: "Sorry, not the things for tapping my heart out, Mary Magdalene," Elizabeth thinks as she unconsciously touches her throat. She resolves to wear pearls the next day on her return to the library. "But only a single strand . . . for the [sake of the] librarians . . . less noisy than tapping my heart out."

"Ma, I brought you some lunch."

Mildly startled, Elizabeth murmurs, "Including some champagne, I hope."

"Oh . . . has it been that kind of day?"

"It's been a lovely day, Penel."

"No champagne; but coffee and a chicken salad sandwich."

"Wonderful. Let's find a bench in the sunshine."

After lunching together, Penelope departs, promising to return to pick up her mother when the library closes. The children are in school and Morti is sailing off the coast of Florida aboard his boat, the *Penel.*

Elizabeth dives back into her research. Resolved to stay focused, she furiously scribbles notes all afternoon until the closing bell sounds and Penelope arrives at the library entrance. On the drive home, unable to break out of the library's spell, Elizabeth thinks back to one of Jim's business trip letters:

> My love, I'd give anything to express in words the way I feel, like you can. But I can't. I can say and mean it more than I ever have that I love you more than I ever dreamed I could. I adore you and this trip (to Buffalo) that might have been a real joy if you had been here has been terrible so far . . . when I get home let's go to the movies two nights a week – that will make it easier not to have a cocktail . . . I did appreciate your letter so. It was the sweetest thing. I might be bad sometimes, but I worship you. Love, love, love, Jim

• • • • •

Home from the FDR Library, Penelope pulls her mother's chair directly in front of a blazing fire and hands her a drink. Elizabeth recalls the turbulent year of 1935. She and Jim are in Europe on behalf of Sonoco. Hitler is on the rise and the Western world order is changing.

Pregnant with their second child, Elizabeth becomes more and more anxious. On returning home, she suffers a miscarriage and falls into depression. Jim decides to take Elizabeth and daughter Penelope to the Chateau Richelieu on Murray Bay in Canada, where his wife can rest and recuperate. Elizabeth's Aunt Aline travels with them to look after the young mother and toddler.

Then in April 1936, the impossible happens. Daddy, Elizabeth's beloved father, dies at the age of 65. When Jim's father died several years earlier, Elizabeth felt she had lost a close and stalwart ally. But it was almost unthinkable to have lost her own father. "Mr. Boatwright," as her mother always called him, had been Elizabeth's unwavering advocate and admirer.

But life continues and she carries on, reflected in this entry from her diary, recalling the summers of 1936 and '37:

> [The first summer] after Jim and I were married, we went for two weeks to the mountains of North Carolina – Blowing Rock, the land of content – and stayed at the Mayview Manor. Mayview was a summer hotel in the grand style where once we might have seen the likes of Henry James or Edith Wharton sitting on the porch in rocking chairs gazing at the heart-breaking mountain view past gardens tumbling down the steep embankments.
>
> The place so charmed us that we began to spend Jim's two-week summer vacations there regularly. One evening at cocktails, in the summer of 1936, we met a delightful literary man, Hirschell Brickell, then a well-known Southern writer and the literary editor of *The New York World*. He, like us, was so delighted by the area that he was considering a plan to start a writers' workshop – modeled on Robert Frost's Bread Loaf [School of English] at Middlebury, Vermont – for the next summer. As he described its possibilities, it sounded so exciting that Jim and I decided to look at a wonderful sprawly old house that an acquaintance of ours owned, and we rented it for the following summer, the summer of '37.

> The house, called Kallalanta, hung over a mountainside as if it were floating in a world of blue space, surrounded by a spectacular sea of mountains . . . as I stood on the steps of that place the first time we saw it, exhilaration enfolded me – a feeling of something wonderful about to begin. A door opening . . . a spark. I knew it. I can still feel it. Blowing Rock played a big part in making me what I am today.

• • • • •

On June 15, 1937, the writing workshop began. There were classes in the old schoolhouse in downtown Blowing Rock, led by Elizabeth and Jim's new acquaintance, Hirschell Brickell. The teachers included poet Theda Kenyon (alumna of the MacDowell Colony), *Saturday Evening Post* editor Stuart Rose, author Margaret Mitchell (who said she found her most valuable research in old trunks and attics), and Clifford Dowdey –the Southern historian and novelist, whose fine Civil War novel, *Bugles Blow No More,* had the misfortune of coming out simultaneously with Mitchell's blockbuster, *Gone With the Wind.*

Jim dutifully came to Kallalanta for the weekends, as did many guests and family members. Blowing Rock was still a summer village then and there were square dances and mountain music on Main Street, picnics on great rocks, and dogs baying in the night for foxes and coons.

In the big house at Kallalanta there was a bowling alley, a billiard table and always music emanating from stacks of records. "Marie, the Dawn is Breaking" played over and over, alternating with "Blue Hawaii." A wonderful cook and a nurse named Harry looked after five-year-old Penelope. Sometimes Jim's mother came up from Hartsville, but mainly it was the members of the writers' group.

Talks and shared readings filled the workshop hours. Lecturers outnumbered students. The days, the nights, the laughs and sighs, the work – it was all inspiring and heady to Elizabeth. She was bewitched by a certain story she was trying to spin into being, and dove into the writing sessions and the thrilling otherness of the artistic life. "Everybody said they liked my work and seemed to realize what I was trying to do before I did," she wrote in her diary. "Every day was a thrill."

It was all foreign to Jim, however, who appeared on Fridays after work and was too polite to admit how relieved he felt when August arrived and the literary lions finally left his lair.

• • • • •

In addition to classes and readings, there was plenty of time for fun and relaxation. One evening, the group pretended to hunt foxes, complete with sound effects of howls and barks. Next door at the inn, guests called to complain of too much yelling and threatened to alert the police.

Elizabeth's brother, P.J. the doctor, would sometimes join them. He knew Clifford Dowdey from their schooldays on opposing football teams, a game which the group played on the lawn of Kallalanta, or pretended to play in the form of touch football. They also rode horses. They even galloped, with and without horses.

There were dances at Mayview Manor to music provided by an orchestra liveried in powder blue suits. When Elizabeth's niece Martha arrived for a visit, she inserted herself into the group and insisted she had seen Margaret Mitchell stretched out in her car for a whole afternoon. Mitchell denied it. Martha did not like Mitchell and neither did Elizabeth. But Clifford Dowdey did, and claimed Mitchell had joined the group just to see him.

Jim loved *Gone With the Wind*, which had been published the year before to rave reviews. But Elizabeth thought Mitchell's characters, especially Scarlett and Rhett, were fools. All the while, she and Clifford Dowdey were growing closer. Her memories of Clifford remained vivid, as evidenced in this journal passage penned years later:

> Once when Clifford and I were standing in Kallalanta's big room, silently, Penelope ran in and Miss Carrie (Jim's mother) followed. Nobody spoke. They left. Kallalanta. Where love flamed for a little while and my heart broke. C. was handsome and tough, a poor boy with street wisdom. Also, a very successful writer at the top of his career – lusty, self-oriented, sensual, voracious – totally concerned with his own feelings . . .
>
> Virginal, I, bewildered and untaught, so unaware of what to

> do . . . I thought I was madly in love with him. I died with pleasure at his touch. How can we ever meet again? C. suggests that I go to Bread Loaf next summer, the summer of '38. I could send Penelope to camp up there.

Many years later, Elizabeth was in Blowing Rock and received a phone call from Clifford. He was nearby. Could he visit? No. She had guests. Instead, she sent a postcard with a picture of the mountains. He replied in a letter the next day:

> To communicate with you in Blowing Rock ("the Land of Lost Content") of all places causes a deep psychological wrench by its bringing alive (as did Proust's taste of the *madeleine*) a period of the most intense emotional experience of my days on earth. Of course, BR was only where it began, and as I think of the place in writing you, I clearly see the details of your house and grounds, even Cousin Martha and Margaret Mitchell (and by the way, what she was doing was visiting me) and what I remember most about that visit was your cousin Martha's deathless line, in the disenchantment following her original awe, "let her stay at home and read *Gone With the Wind"* . . . and a poem you wrote. As well as the "football field" where your brother P.J. and I ran and where I first knew I loved you, and the big hotel dance where we knew we were fatefully, hopelessly in love. I believe I would have fulfilled my potential as a creative writer instead of giving up for straight history if . . . if . . . if . . . so much was through circumstances, mainly your blessed self . . . realize that absolutely nothing can ever equal for me the wonder of having known you . . . that reality is the link between the inner me of 1937 and what remains forty years later. As I look back to evaluate my days it all comes back to You, You, You.

In his letter, Clifford mentioned the following poem, which Elizabeth kept:

Burst cloud!
Beat rain!
Drench the dusty earth again.
Break heart!
Stab pain!
Love has turned her face again!

• • • • •

By the end of the summer of 1937, the workshop was over and Clifford was off to Bread Loaf in Middlebury, Vermont. Elizabeth was determined to join the storied writers' group the following year if she could get in. She wrote a letter to Jim:

> Dearest Jim – I've got a bee in my bonnet and I am deadly serious. I feel I must have a chance to see if I can write. I feel it so hard that I cannot sleep at night and it's worrying me terribly. It will mean study, study, study, and work, work, work and I don't know if you'd be willing for me to throw so much energy outside of our home. Please think about it and if you are not willing for me to take the whole thing as my life work and go after it in my own way, tell me now and I'll try to give it up. Or – don't get after me for neglecting you and Penelope once I've started. I just want to try my wings and if they won't fly, I'll be eternally grateful to you for the chance I've always wanted and never had. If you'll give me a year I'll be content to rest or fall on the results at the end of the year. Please write me as soon as you get this, for I'll do whatever you say. But no power on heaven or earth will ever make me go back to the gossiping, giggly society I've been moving in. Don't think too hard of me. I'll probably get sick again and it will all blow over. But I do want to try. I dread having the girls I invited up here because I have to spend so much valuable time away from my work that I have started. Love always, Elizabeth
>
> P.S. Bring some you-know-whats with you, please. I don't

want a baby till next year. I'm sorry –

That fall there was a letter from Isobel Tozzer, an old New Yorker who had befriended Elizabeth's brother William when he was enrolled in school there. She had also been kind to Elizabeth during her 1929 stay in the city. Isobel had lived in China for years and seemed to know everything. She and Elizabeth kept in touch and Isobel became a "best friend." Following a visit to New York by Elizabeth and Jim, she wrote:

> I want to tell you so much. Perhaps I did seem cynical about your plan (not really, I'm just practicing another hideous Xian virtue called resignation). But I wasn't cynical enough to pass up enjoying your hair, dress, ring and facial, and your shoes. I mention shoes for they were trim, but trim too in a sinister manner – as you encase your toes with perfect fitting shoes (you did say you didn't expect to walk in them), be sure your soul doesn't get fitted too; for there is never a time when you don't have to have it warm and flexible.
>
> I never want to see you gain in brittle beauty. You are using the finest tools for the polishing of manner and mind – travelling and reading and association. But I am not quite certain that you can successfully use the method of a lapidary on your self – a human has to be constantly mobile and outside the static of a gold ring.
>
> I have written for Bread Loaf school literature. Whenever you go next summer to write, remember you are privileged in going and don't use your information in any other way than to pave the path to tolerance and joy for others. How utterly banal this sounds – yet I must say it until you have emerged from a world of self and platitude. If you are an introvert and creative I would hesitate, but you are an introvert playing the game of an extrovert . . .

• • • • •

Elizabeth's diary contains few references to the summer of 1938, except for brief mentions, noting "the year of Munich and Middlebury, Summer School and Bread Loaf Writers Conference, and Clifford and Basin Harbor." She had found a "splendid camp" for Penelope nearby, called Aloha on Vermont's Lake Ely, where Penelope learned to ride.

When Elizabeth arrived at camp to visit on Mother's Weekend, she thought she was dressed perfectly in a pair of tailored shorts. This so embarrassed her little daughter that Penelope burst into tears and begged, "Why can't you dress like a proper mother?" This question was repeated by mother and daughter, like a mantra, for years to come.

Elizabeth's goal at Bread Loaf was to finish the story she began the previous year and had been working on all winter – that of a beautiful mulatto enslaved girl, who was to be the prize for the winner of a grand horse race. She noted on the manuscript: "They liked it! Ted Morrison and Robert Frost!"

In another notation that summer, Elizabeth wrote:

> Saranac, horse races, Eddy Duchin.
> Middlebury Inn – C came
> Old New York Hotel
> Drove all night. Pistol in car
> Alien corn.
> I could not leave. It was not in me to cause so much hurt to
> Jim, so worthy and good.
> Neither could C.

Decades later in 1979, Clifford wrote: "This is an anniversary, a bleak day like those in Connecticut 41 years ago when we could not let go and, for reasons known to you, I could not make the break. Neither could you. Though I remember as if yesterday, straining at the bars."

Elizabeth returned home at summer's end in 1938 and took up her old life again. She wrote:

> To Jim
> Happiness is a tall king
> Gay with power
> Happiness is joy and pain

In an hour.
Happiness is wisdom's folly
Come to flower.
P.S.
Happiness is everything I can bring
To that tall king.

Chapter 7

WIFE AND WRITER

Elizabeth was writing regularly, intensely; trying all avenues, using everything she had. She recalled, "Some things I sent to C. to critique, a few to magazines. C. did not seem as interested in my work as I had begun to expect. Especially my Civil War stories, at least their beginnings . . . neither did the magazines: *Colliers. This Week. The Readers Digest.*"

In real life, she and Jim were busier than ever. Their hectic corporate existence was compounded by demanding social, familial and community obligations. She savored moments when she could escape and gallop across the countryside surrounding Hartsville astride her wild-eyed horse named Baron.

Meanwhile, Jim was working far too hard, planning new products for the approaching war, as well as anticipating opportunities for expansion. He started with 300 employees when he became president in 1931, and now there were 2,000. He also served on the boards of Coker College (founded by his grandfather), the local bank, and various business entities and charitable organizations.

One late December, the following account appeared in *The Hartsville Messenger*:

> On Christmas evening Mr. and Mrs. James Coker III entertained at a lovely dance at their home on Home Avenue [Loblolly Hill]. The entire lower floor was thrown open for dancing. The house was festive with decorations of Christmas greens and candles. During the evening the guests were entertained by the Silver Moon quartet. A buffet supper was served.

Guests included the genial clan of Coker cousins, a number of Boatwright family members, friends from Coker College, and many young Hartsville residents and couples who loved a good party. In spite of everything, namely a second world war on the horizon, it was a happy time for Elizabeth. She recorded in her journal:

> We and our young friends and cousins all laughed a lot; we enjoyed our children and our multitudes of animals. We had bird dogs, chihuahuas, cats, a parrot (named Boney because he bit your finger to the bone if he could), rabbits, cats, Thomas – a little goat with a cart that I continually fell out of, [and] a white pony for Penel. At birthday parties, like us, the children were dressed to kill, each child with its own personal starched nurse. In later years, I saw them clearly and nostalgically in the old faded home movies of another long-ago world.

• • • • •

Certain individuals wove in and out of Elizabeth's life during this time and became her intellectual and spiritual kin. She described a few of these special people in her diary.

> There was Julia Peterkin, who came and lectured at Coker College and stayed with us; the brilliant and outrageous Elliott Springs (of Springs Mills and also a writer, e.g. *War Birds*) was a regular visitor. He and another South Carolina writer stand out plain from the rest of our state fellows in that they did not rely on historical, ethnic or environmental treasures of our state, but reached far beyond it for their inspirations and material. This is not meant to compare James McBride Dabbs' *The Road Home* (Dabbs was professor of English at Coker College) with Elliott's *How to Make a Buck on a Springmaid Sheet* (featuring a matinee idol Indian and a sparsely clad blonde on the cover), though both were world famous creations at the time: appreciations and acknowledgements of the needs and aspirations and glory of individual man, any man.
>
> Dabbs was a quiet man with passionate convictions and prejudices. I sat in on his classes often. As a teacher, he was spellbinding except for the fact that he had no sense of humor. I wondered if many of his students recognized the pearls he cast before them. He was a handsome man, tall and ruggedly

> built. He lived in a little house he called Patchwood on the college campus with his wife Jessie, who was very ill. He wrote of himself on *The Road Home* in the 30s: "I am convinced that we might find the eternal, as Marius the Epicurean felt he had found it, in the mere clinging of human creatures to each other." Through the years, I reveled in Mr. Dabbs' success as he engrossed himself in civil rights, becoming one of its outstanding voices in his books *Who Speaks for the South, Haunted by God* and *Civil Rights in Recent Southern Fiction*.
>
> At the other end of the spectrum, the most prolific of our hunter-poet storytellers was Archibald Rutledge. He was a lovely looking man, over six feet tall, thin and erect. He had brown hawk eyes in a delicate boned face, and though he was aloof and detached, he had a winning manner. He was the epitome of the smooth soft outside, steel inside, gentleman-hunter-naturalist writer who used to ornament our state. I don't think he ever considered me a writer even when I was finally published. To him, I was just another young Coker wife who had clustered around him on Uncle David Coker's piazza to listen to his delightful way of telling stories of his adventures in the woods and waters of the low country.

One of the best friends Elizabeth ever had was a fellow Darlingtonian named Chapman Milling.

> My first memory of him was as a small child when our little school was having an amateur circus evening. Chapman arrived in turban and *djellabah* [a Moroccan cloak] with two live snakes writhing around his neck. He never failed to make an entrance, for he wore many hats: poet, hunter, doctor, historian. Chapman's story of Indian tribes along our rivers, *Red Carolinians*, is a magnificent glimpse of our past.

She cites other close South Carolina writer friends in her diary. Among them was Havilah Babcock, who encouraged Elizabeth to keep plugging away at her writing:

> A writer, teacher, raconteur, Havilah wrote for the leading magazines, and his books were lazy loose accounts of his rambling adventures. He loved nature, and he told me that he never knew what to expect on his jaunts, for nature was more surprising than a woman.
>
> Another vital friend was Samuel Gaillard Stoney, whom I met with his poet wife Frances Frost at a wedding in Charleston in 1931; and I was so excited at being arm in arm with two real life authors that I could hardly keep still during the garden wedding ceremony. His book *Black Genesis* had been published the year before with a foreword by DuBose Heyward, and his knowledge of the Gullah blacks was amazing. Sam acted the part of a bold, bad man and was one of the angels of Charleston historic preservation in its early days. He dashed around the streets of the ancient city on his bicycle, black cape winging behind him, hair and beard flying around his face like feathers. He was a stocky man with quick eyes and a huge voice. He wore baggy unpressed clothes and was impatient and restless at gatherings. Once at a lecture at Coker College, sitting between Jim and me, he took a short nap, jumped suddenly awake, pulled his beard and shouted, "My most exciting evening was when Frances' brother cooked a pot of lobsters on Oyster Bay!" His books *Charleston* and *Plantations of the Low Country* are classics of their kind.

• • • • •

> The decade was ending. The war was coming closer. Our lives would change forever. Meanwhile, a poem I had written was published. I called it "Registrant Unable to Read and Write."
>
> Sing Ho! For Utopia
> When firing shall cease

A CURIOUS HEART

Let's hurry for bundles
For Britain and Greece
We'll feed the French children
On Charlottes and cream
And see that the Chetniks
Find truth in their dream.
Let's send missionaries
to China and Iceland
Knit long, heavy sweaters
for Holland and Poland.

(But what of our brother
who toils in the cotton?
And what of his sister
Whom God has forgotten
His father and mother
Pellagra has broken
The silent mosquito
Leaves death as a token

O! Where is the schoolhouse
To open his eyes?
And who is to rouse him
To dream e'er he dies?)

Utopia! Utopia!

Come with swift precision
But bring us Myopia
Along with our vision!

Chapter 8

THE FORTIES: VICTORY AT LAST

In 1941 Elizabeth gave birth to a son, James Lide Coker IV. The umbilical cord was wrapped around his tiny neck. Big sister Penelope had the measles and was sent away to stay with her grandmother Carrie (Jim's mother). The nine-year-old was angry "as a curly haired boa constrictor deprived of a meal," wrote Elizabeth. Forgiving her family was not easy. To make matters worse, a German nurse named Miss Kleinschmidt was hired to look after Penelope's pink-faced, golden-haired baby brother. "Miss K.," like everyone else, treated James IV like a cherub.

Later Elizabeth commented, "She [the nurse] dotes on little James and me and scorns poor Jim and Penel. They are dark. James and I are fair . . . I'm afraid Miss K. is a Nazi." The nurse stayed on for several months as Elizabeth slowly regained her strength. Letters poured in, including one from Julia Peterkin.

> Dearest Elizabeth,
>
> The news of the arrival of your little son gives me such a thrill of pleasure not only because he is here, but too, because you are safe and sound. And I can make no better wish for him than that he should be like either one of his parents. Bless him and you and Jim.
>
> Much love, Julia

Before long, Elizabeth was fit enough to return to her volunteer post at Hartsville's Byerly Hospital as a nurse's aide. The job helped her understand her brother P.J., a committed physician, and she felt she could have easily followed in his footsteps. In the hospital, a second world war seemed closer than ever.

Elizabeth also resumed writing. She described her progress in a notebook entry:

I was still working on that story that I began in Middlebury. I called it "The Red Filly" and it was about a beautiful light skinned black girl who was wagered and won on a horse race. I showed it to a sort of literary friend, a short square, elegantly dressed blond tank of a woman, who also had the "honor" of decorating all of "our" houses. They were draped with beautiful fabrics and furnished with expensive antiques, heirlooms and classical "faux" furnishings. She had become a fast friend and I loved that she came from New York City. Her name was Lucille Kerfoot and it was rumored that she had met her handsome second husband, then making a living as a palmist, and [that] he read hers at a nightclub in New York, accurately foretelling her future. . .

Lucille had taken a course at Columbia University and she suggested that I accompany her on her next New York buying trip so that she could introduce me to one of her more famous professors – a well regarded writer, critic and teacher, Professor Glenn Mullen. As hoped, he had agreed to read "The Red Filly," and during our meeting, to my delight, he said it was good [enough] to make it into a novel!

Of course, that had been my dream since Bread Loaf, and for a long time I had been writing, rewriting, editing in bits and pieces when I could steal time. Professor Mullen's notes said: "This has a genuine quality of life in it. The era is admirably captured . . . it is too long for a short story, too short for a novelette, but it could be blown up as *My Friend Flicka* was." During the war years Jim was in Washington with the Office of Price Administration and the OPM, whatever they were. Anyway, I had more time, as Jim was away during the week with his dollar-a-year war job.

Aside from our household, we had bantam chickens in the front yard as well as Penel's pony Queenie – Penel and Uncle Bert our ancient yardman took care of them. Thomas the goat was in the back, everywhere were assorted chihuahuas, spaniels, bird dogs, cats, bulldogs. We ate Swiss steak and biscuits and wiener stew (particularly nasty), and sometimes one of our chickens that bare-footed Rosa killed and plucked (not very well, much to Mozelle's disapproval) and fried. We gathered eggs and there were always plenty of greens. Jamesie was an enchanting blue-eyed golden-haired cherub and Penel was our fearless little Elizabeth Taylor. Jim left for Washington on the train from McBee (twelve miles away) every Sunday night and returned on Fridays. In summer, we went to Blowing Rock, renting a different house every year until we built our own beautiful one in 1945.

• • • • •

During this same time, Coker College's annual literary festival was growing in prestige and Elizabeth and Jim agreed to host the lecturers and luminaries at Loblolly Hill. Elizabeth treasured these new friends and their letters of thanks, such as this one from poet and editor Louis Untermeyer:

Dear Elizabeth,

An hour ago I sent off four books to your ménage [some of which Untermeyer had edited and/or introduced] . . .

This is an awkward way of saying what I was unable to tell you in Hartsville: that you gave me a rich – and resuscitating – weekend. Perhaps the Beauty-and-Cutie contest may have heightened my enjoyment. Perhaps the good breakfasts, the debut of Penel in church [her confirmation], and the sight of the swamp cypresses may have had something to do with it. But what was most rewarding was that I had made (I hope) a new friend – and that, as far as I'm concerned, admits of no perhaps.

Thank you again – and may it not be too long before we meet again.

Affectionately, Louis Untermeyer

Elizabeth was trying to find time to fix her story as Professor Mullen had suggested, but she was sidelined by additional concerns. Letters from her friend and former employee, Harold Young (a World War II pilot in the European theater) moved Elizabeth to write a poem entitled "Icarus Toiling in a Garage," based on their correspondence:

How are you standing the stress and strain
Of being at home and at peace again?
"I can't get used to just staying put.
I keep waiting for a call to go out.
It's the idea of staying that gets me down.
Day in and day out in this dinky town.
When you've crossed the country in an hour.
You get filled up with a sense of power.
Soaring from mountains over the sea,
Made an immortal of plain old me.
My wings shone silver in the morning sun
And at evening, of gold dust they were spun.
Then once as I sped through a foggy night
My motor stalled! The plane in full flight,
Crashed to earth. There were ten in my crew
Who'd been with me the whole way through.
Yet when I crawled forth from that burning cone
I saw that of ten – I stood alone.
I felt that God had a finger on me.
All that I'd been and reckoned to be.
But here I lie – oiling a dirty car
When I should be tilting up to a star
For I have exchanged words with the moon
So I keep expecting a call – soon
Oh, I date fancys and drink and scoff.
But I still can't believe that my wings have
dropped off."

• • • • •

Meanwhile, Penelope had been sent off to Chatham Hall boarding school in Virginia. It was not a good fit. Letters flew back and forth:

> Dearest Penel,
>
> Up in my room listening to the Clemson-Carolina game. Would give anything to be there in the dust and noise.
>
> We had a most interesting party. Father Williamson (whom you know I dote on and would almost become a Catholic for) called me Monday afternoon to invite me to a song service at the Catholic church. I went, and who should furnish the "song" but Tito Guizar and his Mexican band.
>
> It was lovely and he sang and looked like an angel. Afterwards we brought [home] the Father, Tito and his wife, plus his manager and piano accompanist, plus Tony and Jimmy (the adorable fairy haberdashers in town) and Uncle Charles and Aunt Tootsie and other cousins. Tito brought his famous guitar and sang and sang and sang, mainly Mexican folk songs. He has just finished three months at the Starlight Roof at the Waldorf, and en route to Palm Beach, he had liked the look of the Lake Park Motor Court and liked the nearby college horses, so he stopped – and like a proper Catholic – had contacted Father W. Da is fine, sends love, had a wonderful time at the party. He is working far too hard.
>
> The score now in the third quarter is Columbia 6, Clemson 0. I do miss you so.
>
> Love, Ma

January 20, 1947, New York:

> Oh Penel, New York has been wonderful. Or rather without little James to nag at me has been wonderful. Thursday night dinner with Marjorie Daingerfield – her new sculptures are her best – and her equally talented husband, Louis Lundean, at the Hotel Des Artistes. Friday, a lovely long dinner and chat with Isobel [Tozzer]. Like I, she wants you to be both happy and educated.
>
> Saturday, Lucille Kerfoot and I went to see "Lady Windermere's Fan" with Cornelia Otis Skinner and beautiful sets and costumes by Cecil Beaton. Sunday, I had a conference with Professor Mullen of Columbia University about my horse story, which I have called "The Red Filly." He insists I make it into a novel and feels that it will not only be interesting, but a real literary contribution.
>
> Da came yesterday and we gave a party at the St. Regis in the King Cole Bar for twelve. Salvador Dali was sitting at another table facing me. He stared (I had on the gold feather hat), then he busily sketched my head. Finally he leapt up, dashed over, kissed my hand and went away muttering "tres jolie, tres gentil, tres tres. . ." (French, dear Penel, in case you didn't know) but he did not give me the sketch. Wurra wurra!

• • • • •

In 1948 Harry Shaw, an old South Carolina friend and admirer who became an important advisor and editor, introduced Elizabeth and her book to a literary agent he knew. The agent, Maxwell Aley, wrote to the author in March of that year after reading part of the reworked manuscript:

> Dear Elizabeth,
> Ruth [Aley's wife and partner] and I feel that you have made a great advance in the structure and pattern and now everything

> depends on a slow, thoughtful working out. Let none of the inherent quality and richness escape you. Both Ruth and I feel you have a chance for an important novel here and we are sure you can do it. Just don't do it too speedily; it will be a slow painful process as all good books are. "Art is a jealous mistress and if you don't give her everything, she kicks your teeth in." Best of luck. Be in touch.
>
> Cordially, Max Aley

That same year, Penelope convinced her parents to let her transfer to Mt. Vernon Seminary in Washington, D.C. Correspondence from Elizabeth to Penelope reveals the author's challenge of balancing family life and writing.

> . . . time will fly. You will be home in no time.
>
> Meanwhile I will have progressed exactly none on my book. I have been visiting Mama (Granny) at her new home in Columbia. She was fine and likes this new place much better than the others.
>
> Crash. Ran downstairs in the middle of the night. Cat had caught bird and was pulling him out of his cage. I managed to salvage the unconscious bit of yellow and warmed it back to a little life. He is hopping about again but I'm afraid one eye is out.
>
> Uncle William is in very bad shape, and I am trying to write letters to people who might help him get a job. So is Da.
> Uncle Duncan died.
> James has impetigo on his little mouth.
> I can't write.
>
> The end. I hope, though the day still has hours to run. I'll go back to see Granny in Columbia on Wednesday, then Friday I have 80 women to tea.

Monday week to New York. We will stay at the Plaza and I am excited about it. That weekend to Mystic to visit the Whites, the Yale-Dartmouth game.

We love you.

Note: Granny died that weekend while I was in Mystic. We got home just hours too late.

• • • • •

In the winter and spring of 1949, as her first book was nearing completion, Elizabeth shared with Penelope the trials and triumphs of the writing life.

. . . Such a wasted fall and winter for me on whom has descended a terrible sense of urgency about not letting precious, precious time slip away. There are so many wonderful, thrilling things to do. If only I'd make an effort. That was the great lesson in *Peter Rabbit*. You remember when Peter got caught in the gooseberry net by his coat buttons and Farmer McGregor was about to catch him – the little birds implored Peter to "make an effort?" He did and everything turned out all right after that . . .

Forgive brief card and don't be too angry at poor me who is trying so desperately hard to be an aspiring clod. I couldn't visit school because of book things that have developed since I have been in New York and I feel I must bend every effort to push it through.
Love, Ma

Dear P – Just now a phone call from Harry the Shaw saying he adores book and all the new stuff! Now he wants us to send it to Bobbs-Merrill. What a relief! Now I can dig in and do 200 pages by mid-May if I have to. I need a secretree most horrendously! My pencils are never sharp, my pens are always

> lost, my files are a mess and my desk is absolutely immoral. And three meals a day. And those dead two hours from noon to 2, and nothing ever to do. I am in fine health, but quite heavy in the butt. I just eat all the time. Da is much relieved not to have to travel just now, but if you get weakly, one of us would surely fly to your aid and comfort. Rushing now to Charlotte to be hostess at the men's camellia show at the American Trust Co. for Frank Dowd. . .
>
> I love the delicious hat and your greeting to a lady just turned the horrible milestone of 40 was quite soothing. However, I'm not sure I've "growed" enough. Mr. W at Bobbs-Merrill was very cross at my revision. Said I was too in haste and that everything was being told from the wrong point of view. VERY desolating to me.

Then in mid-July of 1949, a note arrived from agent Max Aley:

> Dear Elizabeth, as you know we are always doubtful about untried writers, but in your case the merits of even the first draft of the novel spoke for themselves. That is why we have stuck by. I do think you were too hasty in your early revisions, but I have great hopes for the present version, which you are doing more slowly. As you know, I have spoken to Macmillan's and Dutton, and Jim Putnam is waiting. . .

That same month, Elizabeth sent the following letter to a friend:

> I'll never forget what a time I'm having getting Tafra [the matriarch in *Daughter of Strangers*] buried. Her body has been lying upstairs all this hot week because Jim found a snake skin protruding from the radiator grill in the library and had to take down every book and then put them back again (Mozelle refused to help – she cares not for snakes); take down the pictures, take up the rugs, shake them up and of course nary a snake did we find.

I have made so many false starts. I began with a luscious, full-blown heroine. Then in disgust, I destroyed a hundred pages and whisked her back into babyhood. In due course, each chapter, I hope, is a fountainhead of inspiration for the next one. If I even write another book, I will outline my story before I write it and maybe the sloughs of despond and the falling rocks I have encountered wouldn't have tripped me up so. But I was not experienced enough to understand how important it is to outline and re-outline, to plan and plan again. For writing is like any invention – you have to be familiar with the tricks and spills of the trade. Each scene must be as vital and as necessary as the parts of a smooth, running machine.

Vincent McHugh says that "the events of a novel should fit the sense of a whole as an egg fits in its shell." But there is an enchantment that takes hold, like some strange spell, so strong and consumingly interesting that nothing else seems to matter – there is that scary feeling of playing God with your characters, wielding the power to shuttle them in and out of your (and their) life at will.

The worst times are when large black-winged doubts attack me. What assurance do I have that I am not wasting my efforts? Why should I think that anybody would be interested in my little story?

Then along comes a good day when words sparkle and leap from my decrepit old typewriter. My characters take hold of the scene by themselves, I merely follow their actions, and one of those days makes up for all those difficult ones.

Aley wrote again on July 26, 1949:

It's too bad you are not going to be able to do much work on the book this summer. I have, as you know, a strong belief in it, and I am sure you will eventually bring it through and

> have a real success. And don't let your other idea for the next book wait too long. It too has real possibilities.
>
> As you know, I have avoided trying to pin you down to any hard and fast scheme of revision because it seems to me you are a highly creative person and must eventually work out your own final version of this book. Eventually, I want to put it again directly into Jim Putnam's hands. I would like to discuss our future professional relationship when you are next in New York. With kind regards to you and Jim. Sincerely, Max Aley

Elizabeth continued reworking and revising her manuscript through the summer and fall of 1949. She recounted the finale in her journal:

> Work, work, work. In December, at Harry Shaw's instigation, we took the book to Harcourt Brace. They said, in effect: "Give a party, take a trip, you've written a book, put it in a drawer."
>
> That night, we went to El Morocco with Mac and Tania McKenna (Tania was a former Russian dancer), who had become among our best New York friends.
>
> It got late, time to leave, but Jim and Mac insisted that they were going to the city dump for sparklers. They had read this. Somewhere. Tania and I went back to the St. Regis.
>
> The four of us were having breakfast in the sitting room at the beautiful hotel, and Jim said, "Where is your manuscript? Mac knows Charles Van Doren."
>
> I hastily produced it, and the two of us marched jubilantly off.
>
> Not long after these goings on, Van Doren read it and Mac said he was "wild with praise." When we spoke, he advised me to "introduce the hero first."

When I went home, I did . . . and it seemed to turn the tide for me.

The next person who read it was the boss, Elliott Macrae, at Dutton. Not Nick Wredon [the editor].

"It touches my heart," said Macrae. Wredon would never have accepted it. Thus ended 1949.

Chapter 9

THE FIFTIES: BESTSELLING AUTHOR

On January 3, 1950, William Boatwright wrote to his sister, Elizabeth:

> . . . I do believe that a letter from you to the senator would be of inestimable value to me. I have tried to get a job, but to date my head and the proverbial stone wall seem to have a great deal in common. I have constantly run into three different obstacles – first, not being an ex-serviceman (not my fault); second, my age; and third, my record of sobriety is not too hot . . . if I could just get any sort of federal job, I could handle it. I know I could do well in education or agriculture or anything dealing with the public, and God knows, I've got to get something quick.
>
> I am completely broke. We spend no money on ourselves. In fact, we are having a hard time getting enough to eat, let alone clothes. Rosa is working every day, but she only makes $30 a month. I'll tell you the truth. I'm about ready to throw in the sponge. If there is anything you can do for me, please do it now. I believe the senator will listen to you. Your Christmas presents were certainly fine. The pajamas fit to a T and are the only new additions to [my] wardrobe in more than three years.
>
> Love to all of you from your bro, William

Elizabeth responded immediately to her eldest brother:

> William, William, my golden brother; I will do what I can and so will Jim.

And in a note to William the following month, she announced the news of her first book contract:

> . . . Signed a contract with Dutton on February 14th to publish my book. I wanted you to know first. We sail for England tomorrow. With love, Liza

In her diary, Elizabeth recounted the signing in New York:

> On the day Elliott Macrae [president of E.P. Dutton & Company] gave me the contract to sign, I just sat in his office and stared out the window watching the snowflakes swirl down and around the avenue, thinking, "it's always snowing when something terribly important is happening to me. It snowed in March when Penelope was born. Nine years later, it snowed in February when James was born. Another nine years have passed and now this *Daughter of Strangers* is being born in a snowstorm."
>
> "What's the matter, Elizabeth?" Macrae asked.
>
> "I can't remember how to spell my name," I whispered shakily.
>
> "That night of the day I signed the contract with Dutton, Jim and I were the guests of Curtis and Bennie Calder at dinner and the opera. As everyone stood and thunderously applauded "Lohengrin" – at the end of Act I, Scene 1, in the first and most prominent box – I could not bear further excitement and fainted dead away, falling over the front of our box, and was borne gallantly and publicly away by Jim and Curtis.

The next day, aboard *The Queen Mary*, Elizabeth wrote to daughter Penelope:

> Dear Penelope, The orchids you sent are glorious. We got off in quite a whirl. I was still in a daze about book and Europe all in one week. Our cabin was full of flowers, candy, fruit,

books; and telegrams kept pouring in from all sorts and conditions of people about the book. I feel very humble.

Noel Coward is aboard and King Peter of Yugoslavia. K.P. is very young (20ish) and ineffectual looking. Each afternoon I go to the gym at 4:30 and walk primly past the electric horse while Paul Gallico fences with the fencing master. He is marvelous looking and I have tried to catch his eye, but evidently I don't appeal to him. His third wife, the rich and beautiful Princess Garibaldi, is with him. We have met many grand people and are having a fine time.

Now sit and write me all. But don't let your ancient sweetheart Smith fool you. Years is years and they get most depressing. Stay with your own kind and age group. My love, Ma

En route across the Atlantic, Jim also wrote a letter to Penelope:

Dear Penel – the ship is rolling so that it is hard to sit in a chair without holding on [to] something. Ma will write about the old British Cokers of Bicester, who are aboard and becoming our new best friends . . .

We have met a few wheels, one or two cats, and tried to avoid all squares, including the King of Yugoslavia. Thank you for the orchids, if you are the "Tenni" who sent them. I think Ma told you about the horrible event at the opera. It was all very difficult. Love, Da

• • • • •

Once back in the United States, Elizabeth related in her diary the ins and outs of producing the finished volume of *Daughter of Strangers*:

. . . galley proofs came and were read and reread for error; then a copy of the drawing of the [dust] jacket, which turned out

> to be much more fascinating than the Mona Lisa, and finally, the book itself.
>
> Stephen Vincent Benet, after finishing "John Brown's Body," was met in New York by a batch of reporters who asked him how he felt. "Like I've just given birth to a grand piano," he said. Mine doesn't feel like a grand piano, but I think it can pass for a spinet.

There were many favorable reviews of *Daughter of Strangers*, including one by Chapman Milling in *The State* newspaper in Columbia on September 17, 1950, just a few days after its release. "Mrs. Coker knows her South Carolina as only a devoted native can know and love it," Milling extolled. He went on to say:

> Here is romance, but not the sweet tepid romance of lavender and old lace tradition. There is moonlight and even a magnolia or two, but they always appear as a proper background for the blood and bone characters of the story. And these characters include few stuffed shirts. They have all the strength and all the weaknesses of very genuine people.

The following month, Walter Spearman of the *Greensboro Daily News* wrote this review of what soon became a *New York Times* bestseller:

> No one could look less like the author of a controversial book about race relations than the chic Mrs. Coker; but *Daughter of Strangers*, the story of a beautiful octoroon [a colonialist term labeling a person's ancestry as being one-eighth African or Aboriginal] slave girl on an antebellum South Carolina plantation, is no *Gone With the Wind*, which sees only glamor and romance and moonlight in the Old South . . .
>
> "One of the principal themes of *Daughter of Strangers*," explained Mrs. Coker, "is that we must not be so bound by the traditions of our ancestors that we refuse to face the problems of

Elizabeth Boatwright, age four.

Elizabeth and James with baby Penelope in Hartsville.

Elizabeth writing.

Elizabeth (second from left) at a writers' conference in North Carolina.

James IV and Penelope.

Christmas in Hartsville.

Clifford Dowdey.

Elizabeth with publisher Elliott Macrae
of E.P. Dutton and Company.

Elizabeth in Egypt.

Elizabeth in Mexico.

Elizabeth in Mexico.

Elizabeth and Penelope in Indonesia.

Dancing in Indonesia.

Elizabeth receiving her Doctorate from Converse College.

With Penelope in East Hampton, N.Y.

Costume party dressed as Queen Elizabeth.

On the hammock with James IV and granddaughters Eliza and Samantha.

Dust jacket for *Daughter of Strangers*, 1950.

Dust jacket for *Blood Red Roses*, 1977.

Portrait by Alexander Brook.

Elizabeth at home with James Lunn.

Elizabeth on her Corvette.

Portrait by Molly Bishop.

With granddaughter Eliza.

Bestselling author.

Elizabeth with William F. Buckley, Jr.

Induction into South Carolina Hall of Fame, 1992.

> our own day and continue injustices to a minority race simply because we inherited them from the past . . ."
>
> . . . the book has already been selected by the Fiction Book Club for October distribution to 90,000 readers and possibly to an additional 100,000. Its advance sale to bookshops was an unusually high figure of 18,000, and New York booksellers have reported that it is selling better in New York than any other first novel.

Another North Carolina journalist – present at a book launch for *Daughter of Strangers* – described its captivating author as wearing "a broad brimmed hat matching her forest green costume and a gardenia corsage." The reviewer elaborated on the novel and how it came to fruition:

> The book depicts the emotional struggles of a beautiful young octoroon girl who was transported out of a sheltered life in old New Orleans to a life of slavery on a South Carolina plantation.
>
> Background material for the novel, Mrs. Coker said, was gathered in the University of South Carolina library, in addition to her own Caroliniana collection, which is quite large in itself. "Except for the horses," she added with a smile. "That came out of my own experience. I just adore horses . . ."
>
> Questioned as [to] a possible solution to the South's racial problems, Mrs. Coker said emphatically: "I believe tolerance is the only answer." Her novel gives credence to that statement.

Up north, critics also looked favorably on the book. A review by Coleman Rosenberger appeared in the *New York Herald Tribune* on October 15, 1950:

> *Daughter of Strangers*, a story of slaves and great plantations in South Carolina in the years before the Civil War, is a costume romance of more than usual competence – an imaginative narrative which remains within the bounds of the plausible, a

> novel which shows careful research and attention to its writing . . . Mrs. Coker has written an interesting, full-flavored historical novel of her native South Carolina.

• • • • •

On the front flap of the dust jacket of the first edition – which sold for three dollars in 1950 – *Daughter of Strangers* was described as "a novel of many and varied emotional tempests . . . a superbly panoramic view of life on several social levels in the antebellum days of South Carolina." The jacket copy went on to say:

> The gay, relaxed society of the plantation owners, the formal round of the Charleston "season," the prevailing code of honor which patterned the lives of the owners and the turfmen, the excitement of training and racing horses, the traditional dueling by which affairs of honor were settled – these are all in sharp contrast to the lives of the Negroes upon whose labor the ornate existence of the plantation rested.

In conclusion, the blurb offered this observation:

> Slavery is shown in all its aspects, from that of the ivory-skinned octoroon favorites, maintained in luxury in New Orleans, to the staunchly respectable society of free Negroes in Charleston, and the misery and courage of the simple-hearted field hands, house servants, trainers and boatmen.

Elizabeth was not only exploring the historic reality of enslavement in her first novel, but other interracial realities as well, according to South Carolina literary scholar Tom Johnson. *Daughter of Strangers* focused on "such critical social matters as miscegenation (race mixing) and, at least by proxy, with the long-practiced but mainly secret and silent phenomenon of 'passing' (the attempt by a person of color to pass as white)," Johnson states. "This brings the novel right into the 20th century, as these issues were being discussed and considered more and more by Americans, particularly in the idealistic post-World War II years, and especially in the South – where miscegenation was generally forbidden by both custom and law."

Elizabeth would later comment on the fact that the publication of another modern fictional treatment of slavery and miscegenation preempted the adaptation of *Daughter of Strangers* into a film. As Johnson explains, "Although Robert Penn Warren's novel *Band of Angels* was not published until five years later, it was the one that Hollywood chose to adapt for the screen. The movie 'Band of Angels' came out in 1957 and starred Clark Gable and Yvonne De Carlo. Newcomer Elizabeth Boatwright Coker couldn't compete with an older and more established writer in this regard."

Nevertheless, Johnson places Elizabeth squarely "in the vanguard, a decade before the formal beginning of the civil rights movement, of other writers and artists willing to take the risk and put themselves and their art on the line to address racial discrimination, champion tolerance and justice, and present the truth of history – even aspects of its very dark Southern side."

Johnson also notes countless references to Gullah in *Daughter of Strangers* – a distinct African American culture that developed along the South Carolina coastal plain beginning in the 17th century. Unique language patterns and vocabulary, cookery, music, spirituality and customs continue to this day among the Gullah people. Elizabeth no doubt became familiar with Gullah culture in childhood, especially during lengthy stays with her aunt on the May River in Bluffton. The author employed Gullah speech and traditions throughout *Daughter of Strangers,* as some of the novel's principal characters were members of the Gullah community.

• • • • •

Shortly after publication of *Daughter of Strangers*, Elizabeth engaged a new literary agent, Naomi Burton of Curtis Brown, Ltd. "She is said to be first rate," the author reported. "[and] she has read a first draft of the next book!" Burton's initial letter to Elizabeth was encouraging:

> I have read the first part of the new manuscript of your second book [*The Day of the Peacock*]. I do realize that this is a first draft and I expect Nick Wredon at Dutton told you the same thing – namely to watch out for your writing getting

> too flowery here and there. I wish your Annie was not quite so repulsive, but perhaps I am unfair. Keep working! I am delighted on the whole. Sincerely, Naomi

On the inaugural book tour for *Daughter of Strangers* in the fall of 1950, Elizabeth wrote to Penelope, then a student at Sarah Lawrence College, that "the whole thing is now a three-ring circus." She went on to say, "I was the honor guest at a luncheon in Atlanta with Zasu Pitts and Mrs. Freeman, wife of the executive head of Paramount Pictures. Don't swoon. They vow to see that *Daughter* gets to H'wood. Maybe you can go too!"

Once back in Hartsville, Elizabeth sent another letter to her daughter:

> Dear P, My life has been hectically dull this week past. I have gotten so used to taking flight and rushing around that staying home has been strange; and annoying James, of course, has taken this week to vomit every day. Hordes of visitors have poured in; I have had a cold, and Miss Coker College Taylor – who has been staying with me – has proved feeble, deaf and chattery. I will be glad when Da comes home from business in Manchester so I can take off once again . . . Call the St. Regis and see when *The Queen Elizabeth* docks and plan to have dinner with Da that night.
>
> Monday, I speak in Darlington. Tuesday, Aunt Susie takes me over and I speak to the women of Greenville (why do they keep the men away?) at a dinner and autograph . . . so I won't be home when poor Da gets here. The cost of book writing! Friday – Winston Salem; Sunday – Greensboro.
>
> My love always, Ma

Later, after the dinner and book signing in Greenville: "Greenville turned out to be one of the nicest affairs so far. Aunt Susie managed me most expertly, even making me pin up the front of my navy satin dress because it was "far too low for Greenville . . . "

The Greenville News reported on the event in the next morning's newspaper, under the headline "Elizabeth Boatwright (Coker) pleases," by Lutie McGee, who wrote:

> She appeared before a large audience to talk about her book, which is creating a sensation everywhere. A woman of charm and good looks, she made a marked impression on her hearers . . . South Carolinians feel a particular pride in claiming this outstanding novelist who has brought honor to herself and state through one of the most unusual books of the times. It is her first, but all readers are eager for her other contributions to the literary world.

A natural raconteur, Elizabeth enjoyed her many speaking engagements and book signings, and granted countless interviews. She connected easily with readers and sought out friendships with fellow writers of the era. While also a talented poet, it was the historical novel that best combined her interest and skill in historical research and storytelling. Beneath each book's overlay of romanticized plot lines and adventure, there was solid, fact-based research. Elizabeth found inspiration in old diaries and letters, as well as her travels. She explains in her journal how she drew on the rich, complex history of her home state:

> Growing up in South Carolina prepared me physically, emotionally, morally, intellectually and spiritually and filled me with enough determination and ambition to climb up to the top of the world. I liked it up there! So I stayed. And that's where I am – right this minute – on top of the world!

In the midst of Elizabeth's euphoria, a note arrived from Clifford Dowdey. Staying near the Blue Ridge Mountains of Virginia, he poured out his thoughts and feelings:

> I am in a fine hotel in the country and look down a green hillside like the view from that Kallalanta house in Blowing Rock. Perhaps because I can see the Blue Ridge it all seems

> very close. "Marie" was the song for us then, and "Blue Hawaii." They still are. But "Volveras" is how I think of you: you will return because I desire you. With my blessed mother, you are the most important element in my life. That means long days, empty nights, but you are always there. There have been lapses – and there was first together, then a lapse, then together for a moment in New York – so, first together, parallel, then apart, now again together. In this deep thirst, I have learned to believe, the belief is you and it will always be there . . . because for the quick hours I had you to myself. God bless you, my love, Clifford

Upon receipt of Clifford's letter, Elizabeth noted in her diary: "Not one mention of the book. Well, I guess I didn't mention his either. I guess we are mining the same territory in a way."

• • • • •

The following year on July 4, 1951, Jim was in Europe on business and Elizabeth declared in a missive to her husband, "There are fireworks in my heart!"

> Dear Jim, I JUST THIS MINUTE WROTE THE LAST WORDS OF THE NEW BOOK! HURRAY! And I'll get it mailed and sit and chew toenails until I hear if it appeals to Mr. Nick Wredon at Dutton. It worked out to be a long violent strike, and I wish you could have been here to scream with horror over certain passages over the mill, which I have probably done all wrong. At any rate, the nights I have spent over the typewriter until 12 or 1 have borne fruit and the tomato sandwiches have been nourishing, so I have been in good health and spirits.
>
> My neighbor has come over and interrupted me every day whining, "I don't see why you work like that when you don't have to. Come on over and play bridge with the girls and

> me" . . .
>
> Be a good boy. I have missed you frightfully; but with my long, uninterrupted hours and James at camp, I have finished book ahead of schedule. I love you very much and will be glad for our cozy evenings by the air conditioner in the library once more.
>
> Devotedly, Liz

Then on August 30, 1951, Elizabeth sent this note from Blowing Rock to her beloved aunt:

> Dear Aunt Reitta, My summer has been the department of utter confusion. Jim and Penelope returned from Europe the end of July; then Penel appeared up here for horseshow weekend with a house party of 10 wild hoodlums who proceeded methodically to wreck all in sight. She rode a young Irish horse which had never hunted before in the show and won all the hunter classes with him. Then on Sunday night, she took her 10 guests to the horse show ball dinner and stepped on a piece of ice dropped on the floor and broke her leg.
>
> I went with Inglis Fletcher the next week to a writers conference in Cherokee, N.C. We had a grand time. We joined Carl Sandburg, James Street, Francis Grey Patton, Caroline Miller, lots of newspaper people etc. [and] John Selby (*The Hucksters*) . . . we spent three days chatting and drinking and having outrageous fun.
>
> Then a wire from Nick Wredon at Dutton to rush to New York and sign the contract for my new book, *The Day of the Peacock*. I had no rewriting to do and, the preliminaries over, it has gone blithely to the printer from whence it is supposed to emerge in February. I've never been so pleased and delighted . . .

Meanwhile, William Heinemann of Melbourne, London and Toronto was preparing to publish *Daughter of Strangers* in England. Not long afterwards, Dell issued a paperback edition. Two decades later, Bantam Books published another softcover version – issuing four printings in a single year.

• • • • •

Elizabeth's second book, *The Day of the Peacock,* was released by Dutton in 1952. Set in an early 20th century South Carolina mill village, and told through the lives of those whose existence depended upon "the most modern spinning plant in the New South of today," the novel explored the struggle between old wealth and new labor. The textile mill of the postbellum era brought industrialization to the agricultural South; and with it, economic and social transformation. A review by Chapman Milling appeared in *The State* shortly after the book's release:

> *The Day of the Peacock* epitomizes all the conflicts of the New South . . . All those conflicts are competently handled without any of them getting too big for the author, whose mastery of her subject is complete . . .There's one thing about Elizabeth Coker's writing. You simply can't put it down. This reviewer admits that he may be a trifle prejudiced in her favor, but one of these days she'll be ringing up a Pulitzer Prize.

The Kirkus review that appeared on March 1, 1952 expanded on Milling's assertions that the book "epitomizes all the conflicts of the New South" and demonstrates the author's "mastery of her subject:"

> A conveniently planned, deliberately detailed chronicle of South Carolina's cotton and tobacco empires, of the aftermath of wealth and power as it touched – and tarred – the next generation. For Jay Bruton – second and favored son of proud, driving Royal Bruton – defies his father to buy the old Peacock place where he plans a mill of his own, marries coarse, insolent Annie Shamrock for the tobacco money she has inherited, and shows his father that rayon is the fabric of the modern world. His unhappiness with Annie is offset by

> the meeting with Katherine, the daughter of a dedicated labor organizer; but the infiltration of Communism brings violence to them all when Royal Bruton has a stroke during the riot at the plant, Katherine's father is killed by the Party, and Annie – trying desperately to hold her husband – dies in an accident along with an agitator . . . A rather synthetic alignment of familiar faces, pertinent pressures and predictable situations.

• • • • •

The summer of 1952 brought unspeakable tragedy. Elizabeth wrote this brief account in her journal:

> My brother William shot himself to death in his bedroom in the house where we grew up in Darlington. His oldest daughter found him when she came home from school.

Not long afterwards, Elizabeth sent a letter to her next-door neighbor Arabel Rogers in Hartsville.

> Dear Arabella,
> Your letter about William was wonderful. You expressed so definitely and clearly the way my heart was feeling. My brother P.J. and I were both more upset by our brother's death than by either of our parents. I think the tragedy and unhappiness of his life was so shockingly revealed to us in the final desperate act that was his. As a child, I felt so lucky in having such a sweet, kind older brother . . . and those are the memories of him that I can keep . . .
>
> Bless you, my dear, for holding out your comforting hand to me.
>
> Love, Elizabeth

The following year, in June of 1953, Penelope married one of her theater professors from Sarah Lawrence College. Elizabeth described the newlyweds: "He [John Blankenship] is a Midwesterner, in his mid-thirties – tall, poor and dear – a talented, creative man, a set designer. She is a beautiful, spoiled baby; also very determined."

Elizabeth expounded in a missive to a friend on the elaborate wedding at the Coker family home (Loblolly Hill) in Hartsville:

> We pull out all the stops. We engage the Bishop, tie magnolias in the trees, hide wind-up birds in the bushes, build a porch, display hundreds of presents on the dining room table. Poor Jim has wry neck. His head keeps turning away. Is it because of this marriage? He is going to Riggs [the Austen Riggs Center] after the wedding. Riggs [is] in Stockbridge [Massachusetts] near where Penel and John will spend the summer, as he [John] is designing for the Tanglewood operas. Jim will visit them for several weeks.

Thank-you notes flowed in afterwards. Mary Shipp (Baker), Elizabeth's roommate at Converse and in New York, wrote from her home in Sumter:

> Dearest Lib,
> It was an enchanting wedding and Penelope looked the way all brides are supposed to look – and don't. I loved it all. The lilies in the church around the exquisite stained glass windows, the cool fragile greenery, and all those candles. It was just enough, and so right. All weddings ought to take place at 8pm.
>
> Penelope had on THE dress. I don't think I'll ever forget it. Oh, how beautiful she was, her face framed in rose ponts . . . and I highly approved of your white organdy and yellow taffeta job. Was it Nettie's? Hattie's? Sophie's? [American fashion designers Nettie Rosenstein, Hattie Carnegie and Sophie Gimbel] Anyway, whosoever it was, I was mad about it . . . and Meg, my very observant and smart cook wanted to know this morning what Mrs. Coker wore on her little Cinderella feet. Anyway, it was good to shake the cobwebs out of my brain,

> drink champagne in your back garden, the loveliest spot in South Carolina, and see so many interesting people – particularly so many of our old Darlington friends. It all brought back memories of those nice twenties, forever gone, alas.
>
> Here's a big wish for *India Allan* to top all the fall bestseller lists. You stimulate me so and I can let down my literary hair with you . . .

• • • • •

Elizabeth was spending much of her writing time in Charleston working on a new book. There was no better place to delve into historical research than the Holy City. She related one of her many trips there in the early 1950s:

> I met R – of course I knew who he was, the legendary aristocratic breaker of hearts – in fact, I knew the owners of many of those hearts. But when I arrived at the Charleston threshold of a mutual friend at the identical time he appeared, he enchanted me then and throughout the party; and he was most attentive, to the irritation of several of the other guests, including a photographer from New York. He wrote later that I "did delight my vision and all of my other sensibilities, and has ever since and will always – she [Elizabeth] is a great beauty of noble heart and mind and I do greatly adore and admire her . . ."
>
> After the party, he began to write, always in his own old-fashioned patois. There would be one-line notes on a newspaper clipping, a feather, a picture, poems – his and others. And once, shortly after the party, when a little time passed without a note or a clipping, I sent him a picture of a pre-Raphaelite lady in a red cloak gazing forlornly out her window at the knights gathered there. I wrote:
>
> "Can only assume that aggressive Yankee lady photographer has stolen you away! Or my friend Mrs. McGowan, or worse.

> The next set of whitened bones to wash up on the beach will be mine. And there will be those who nod their heads and say 'Poor girl, she was told he was fatal.'
>
> "But oh, how lovely it was to be able to look at you again . . ."

R replied on the same page: "Oh why, oh why, the red queen not realize she do have a noncomparable truelove that would not swap her for the world . . . (destroy)"

Elizabeth reflected, "And I did realize it, although there was never a question then or later of any change of status. I had my wonderful life with Jim. He [R] had his. We never forgot the anniversary of our meeting, and there were many, even past the silver 25th."

Later Elizabeth expressed her feelings for Jim, Clifford and R – her "three loves" – in the following poem:

> From one I learned the kindness of the world,
> The softness and wisdom of the weak;
> The tender ways that happiness uncurled
> Like yellow lilies in a marshy break.
> Another taught me poetry and grace;
> The sound of music on a starless night;
> How Judas trees could resurrect a place
> And clouds can hail a woodlark in its flight.
> But with the third I found white fire under
> Relentless lips: I found that a caress
> Could link the heavens and the earth in wonder
> And make the sun seem dull in loveliness:
> Three loves have made my life both swift and strong
> Fulfillment echoes through me like a gong.
> Three loves – three loves – three.

• • • • •

In October 1953, Elizabeth's third book, *India Allan,* was released and dedicated to her aunt Reitta Boatwright. Named a Doubleday Book Club selection, it became a *New York Times* bestseller by Christmas. An English edition appeared in 1955, published by Robert Hale in London, followed by a Bantam paperback two decades later that would go through five printings.

"Mr. Gittman of Gittman's [Book Shop] in Columbia put on a grand publication day party," according to Elizabeth. "So many activities whirled around the book that I was like a dervish trying to keep balance. The book did well, as [there] was a book club selection, [then] number one on the *New York Times* bestseller list by Christmas."

The tale involved extensive research by the author on a critical period in South Carolina history: the years from 1850 to 1876 following the death of John C. Calhoun and the onset of secession and the Civil War, through Reconstruction to Wade Hampton's election as governor. The setting ranges between Charleston, White Sulphur Springs in West Virginia, and the town of Edgefield, S.C. Specifically, *India Allan* depicts a society family in the throes of dealing with a daughter's elopement, while at the same time exploring the social and cultural distinctions between Charleston and South Carolina's backcountry.

A special feature of *India Allan* is Elizabeth's intermingling of her fictional characters with prominent South Carolina figures of the day – such as Wade Hampton, Governor John Manning, James and Mary Boykin Chesnut, Francis W. and Lucy Holcombe Pickens, Franklin Moses, Calbraith Butler and Martin Gary.

Once again, Elizabeth was lauded for her ability to vividly portray fully developed, compelling characters amidst the prevailing political and social climate of the day. As one reviewer noted:

> Colorful characterization and a plot that moves consistently and successfully through some 26 years of South Carolina's most exciting history, bring Elizabeth Boatwright Coker another bouquet from the public that prefers definite actors to vague participants, and external events to introspective analysis . . .
>
> Mrs. Coker is to be commended for using a mass of research as the background for the lives of her people, the most important being India Allan, her husband and his family, her son, her father, and her old Negro nurse. Numerous familiar person-

> ages are presented; but their purpose is to push the plot along, not to retard or overcome it.
>
> Yet, on the whole, there is an appreciation of the era – the Civil War and its subsequent so-called Reconstruction. The book itself covers the 26 years between the death of John C. Calhoun in 1850 and the election of Wade Hampton to the governorship in 1876.
>
> In minor roles some of South Carolina's notables appear, such as Wade Hampton; Lucy Holcombe or 'Lady Pick,' the wife of Governor Francis Pickens; their daughter Douschka; M.C. Butler, and Martin Gary. All these move in and out of the pages to support the authenticity of the author's story. Throughout the novel there is this continuation of accent on the fictional phase, yet withal it is pervaded by a sense of real occurrence.
>
> Very often Mrs. Coker comes up with a memorable bit of writing, deserving quotation. "Was she hissing or was she talking?" is one revealing remark. Another one to recall is ". . . the one thing to be dreaded is meeting the professional Southerner on a holiday."

• • • • •

The stamp cost three cents on a thank-you note Elizabeth received in 1953 from journalist and author William Olson recalling his encounter with the famous author and her husband. The Cokers had recently hosted a gathering of writers at their mountain retreat.

> Pass the Blowing Rock sign. Swing to the left past the Horse Show grounds, go up a graveled road flanked by rhododendron, and under a *porte cochere* of a large summer mansion of wide, weathered cypress. A gracious welcome. And we find ourselves in a big, sumptuous warm-colored living room, vast

stone fireplace, paintings, trophies, a showplace at once a home. A magnet draws us out to the porch, to the dazzle of space and sharp design of mountain and mountain, stretching the eye. Just for us, the heavens have washed the afternoon mists away. Old Grandfather Mountain fairly jumps at you. The valleys are purple and green and blue. If we leap from the porch, we could float forever.

It's good, that hubbub of iconic voices (belonging to Inglis Fletcher, Paul Green, Legette Blythe, Walter Spearman, Kermit Hunter, Harry Golden, Burke Davis, Chalmers and Alice Davidson, Lambert Davis, Jonathan and Lucy Daniels, among others) retrieves us from out of the dream. In the outskirts of this Fairyland, the voice of youthful James gives a whoop. He doesn't give a fig about the talk of writers. The conference comes to order and we hear of new techniques for writing books: you slip a mike to an old lady doctor, then transcribe the record. Simplicity, thy name is art.

For brain fog at the stroke of six, what better cure than strolling to the warming bar for a scotch? Voices full and hearty blend and struggle. Unseen is the magnetic field of the Cokers' hospitality, the friendly *sine qua non.*

The world is good, the sun is setting, and languor is upon us. But we remove to the porch and the chorus swells again. Yes, goodness is all, not beauty or truth, as Somerset Maugham has said. But I must not be the last to leave. And there is my most courteous host of the sparkling eyes and the good square face, and nearby his wife – the lovely vision, that floats on ethereal slippers.

• • • • •

The 1953 *India Allan* book tour took Elizabeth to Virginia for more speechifying and dinners. She recorded her stay in Richmond in amusing detail.

One [memorable moment] was when the great Elliott Macrae of Dutton walked into Becky Williams' hall in Richmond [Becky Williams wrote *The Vanishing Virginian*, published in 1940 and made into a movie two years later] and seeing me surrounded by a circle of mostly males – and interesting ones at that – [Macrae] determined that after all, he was the real celebrity and would waste no time proving it. He's a cocky little man, looking like the Shah of Iran's slightly older brother, and has the terrier quality of little men: yap-yap-yap! Look at me! See what a fine fellow I am!

He talked all the time telling everybody: "Yes, I'm a publisher. I feel books here (he tenderly lays his hand over his heart) – inside. I'm intuitive. I know. That's how I am able to buy so much better books than my editor or anybody else's editor." This continued until we went to the dinner where he regaled the audience (supposed to be guests, and I was supposed to be the author all this affair was for; but so far no mention of *India Allan* or me, except as a pet) with his VMI [Virginia Military Institute] days and what a fine fellow he was and how even then he knew things (hand over heart) here – inside.

By this time, I felt as I used to when Mama went on a talking spell, and I began to flirt outrageously with the young man on the right, a good friend of Jim's and mine, and being just as damned collegiate as my supposed sponsor.

The next day, October 26, I went to the radio station where Polly Daffron immediately put me at ease. She called to mind things that had happened on past October 26s, and that reminded me that Mama died on this date, and I remembered the awful flight my beloved brother James and I had trying to get home from [up] north. It was good that we were together. Later, Polly gave me some pointers for the Mary Margaret McBride program that I was to do the following Monday.

Then there was breakfast with some women's page editors, and book signings at two big stores . . . I was fading fast, and went back to my hotel room and listened for a loved voice on the phone, but it didn't ring. So, womanlike, I took a bath, lay down for a while and tried not to think, then put on my Nettie Rosenstein pale cashmere suit and a big cream-colored picture hat and fixed my hair low and looked very smart and a bit on the wan side, which always helps.

The mighty Macrae appeared as we went upstairs to join the crowd at the luncheon. I had fetched along from home Pank Coxe, my age, a Southern belle of the twenties, who found E. Macrae stimulating and fed his ego sufficiently . . . And suddenly and otherwhence HE (Clifford) was there and we just simply kissed each other and then everything was all right and the little man with the yap-yap didn't annoy anymore and I was seated between Clifford and Ed Hyde and we all laughed and it was all good and who cared when Macrae announced that the reason he published Mickey Spillane was so that he could afford to publish Becky Williams and me, and wouldn't everyone like to hear how he got into the publishing business?

Then Clifford confessed that he hadn't read my book because he's heard it was all about the Civil War (his territory, he thought) and I said not only that, but your other territory, Virginia too, and he said "Oh, NO" and then we all roaaared with laughter and everybody teased everybody and nobody listened to how the Macrae started publishing books, and then Macrae suddenly discovered Pank and it was mutual admiration, because Pank felt as if she was the celebrity of the day and the Macrae KNEW he was and I was in a cloud of vapor because HE was beside me and we were laughing together and it was a warm good feeling and darn if I didn't find myself mouthing my publisher's own words – "I know for I just feel it inside" – then lunch was over and I was very tired. Then more people came in afterwards, and I signed books, and they asked me to say a few words, and HE was back, and very pale, so I had to do well; so I told a couple of jokes and thanked Peggy O'Neill for having launched my first book, *Daughter of Strangers,* and for having this party. Then I thanked Elliott Macrae for having felt me (horrors – what am I saying?) I mean for "feeling" *Daughter* and discovering me. I hastily introduced him, thinking now he will tell them how much I mean to Dutton, etc. But little men don't do things like that, so he said as how he would never forget the first time he saw me, and how charming I was, and that Becky Williams had promised him her new manuscript soon, and that today he had discovered another charming woman, Mrs. Coxe, who was chaperoning Mrs. Coker and then sat down, and finally it was intermission.

There was a wonderful party at Ann Johns' house. I was tired and felt fragile, but I came slowly to life until Macrae said, "You'd like to know how my father, himself a Richmonder, made his way in the world."

So then nobody else said anything for a long time, and all I heard was yap-yap-yap, but it didn't bother me. We left around eleven and Macrae said "Why don't we drop Elizabeth first – I know she is exhausted, and then we can take Pank home."

And he asked me if there was anything he could do for me (the eleventh hour, no less) and I said yes. I need a dose of Milk of Magnesia and would they stop at a drugstore. They were all closed, and with regrets, Elliott Macrae leaned out to kiss me goodbye.

Pank and I flew out of Richmond early the next morning. I felt as if I had been ill for a long, long time and was going to be well when I finished this weak stage. I felt as if a benediction had been said to something that had been very beautiful in my life. And I breathed a goodbye to Clifford and I guess Macrae went back to New York. I wouldn't know.

• • • • •

That same year, Elizabeth was invited to be on the Mary Margaret McBride Midday Show in New York City – the most popular interview program in America. Listeners numbered from six to eight million daily, and McBride was referred to as "The First Lady of Radio." Elizabeth recalled the interview.

> Appearing that day were P.G. Wodehouse, who had a new *Jeeves* book; Guy Bolton of "No No Nanette;" Lord Donegal, the Irish nobleman who had penned the history of Ireland and – whisper – was the current boyfriend of *Washington Post* columnist Sheilah Graham. Guy Bolton, a kindred spirit from Savannah, saw my nervousness. "They are all cutthroats," he whispered. "All out to get the spotlight. Think up something outrageous, and when she tosses you the ball, run with it. Don't give it up. Tell all . . . be a cutthroat too . . . the object is to be invited to stay on and have a private interview for national distribution . . ."
>
> What had happened recently? P's wedding, of course. So why not tell about tying magnolias on the trees, and the wind-up birds in the trees, and the frogs brought in from Black Creek to serenade each other around the swimming pool, and the New York theatrical people listening to old Uncle Bert singing gospel songs on the front porch, and P refusing to leave; then move on to courthouse square in Darlington on Red Shirt Day . . . anyway, I won.

On the same day as the Mary Margaret McBride interview, Elizabeth received a letter from her devoted friend Isobel Tozzer of New York:

> Liz dear:
>
> You are good to think of sending me a copy of your new book in the midst of your increasingly fabulous life; and even should I hate every darned description, I'd still love the "from Lizzie" part on the fly leaf. Of course, I'm proud as punch of your public self; but it is as froth compared to my real gratitude for the INNER you, which is more and more able to dominate your living. And whatever fun and glory attaches itself to you as an author, enjoy to the hilt. Whatever discipline and self-searching and revelation have come to you in creating the story – cherish as a reward honestly won.
>
> Devotedly, Isobel (and who is this Reitta Boatwright you have dedicated your book to?)

The year 1953 also afforded Elizabeth an invitation to appear on "This I Believe" with Edward R. Murrow. By then, *India Allan* was a Doubleday Book Club selection and had been bought by an English publisher. Murrow hosted "This I Believe" from 1951 to 1955 on the CBS Radio Network. The show encouraged both famous and everyday people to write short essays about their personal motivations in life and read them on the air. "This I Believe" became a cultural phenomenon that stressed individual belief rather than religious dogma. Its popularity developed and then waned during the era of Senator Joseph McCarthy and the Cold War. Here is what Elizabeth told Murrow:

> When I was 16 years old, I suffered a terrible blow on the right side of my face that broke my cheekbone, cracked my jawbone in several places, and knocked out my front teeth. The first time the doctor let me look at the grotesque image of myself in the mirror, I fainted. But fortunately, I had a sensible, as well as a loving, father who refused to let me hide myself in the back room but took me driving, in our red Overland touring car, through the streets of our little town, as soon as I was able, forcing me to make the effort to smile and speak pleasantly

to everyone we met. This was a hard thing to do; but harder was the learning to greet each day, as well as to meet each day, to realize that the world was not a cushion to be sat on, but a challenge that must be met. Accepting this has helped me build a sustaining faith and a state of mind that has, ever after, given me the fortitude to stand up and face cruel disappointment and the loss of many whom I loved most dearly.

By not shrinking from people, I have always been singularly rich in friends of all ages. I think, in my desperation, I came to believe that it was up to me to go the mile beyond the other mile in order to secure and hold friendships. Of course, I was mistaken in such an idea, but that extra mile has held some of the sweetest experiences life has offered me. Too, it has made me more generous of sharing myself with others, teaching me to regard each person as precious and vital to me. People, in themselves, became important, not just humanity in the abstract – they are easy to love, for they make few personal demands – but also the ones who came alone, knocking at the door of my heart to let them in for comfort.

I believe in the blessed balm of laughter. Even laughing in the dark is a more melodious sound to our Creator than whimpering over our fears and incapacities. By developing an innate sense of humor, I have passed smoothly through many situations that would have undone me had I tried to destroy them with criticism and caustic comments. If we place the proper value on laughter, we learn to believe in tolerance, which, in the end, is my strongest credo. I believe in tolerance of races, of the weak ones, the different, and even of those who have climbed higher than ourselves.

As the years have passed, medical skill has worked wonders. The face that looks out at me from my mirror has become more like the face remembered from childhood. I suppose it is my adjustment to life that I have become accustomed to. I do not mean that I have not "kicked against the pricks," as St. Paul did. My adjustment has consisted of kicks aplenty. Yet today, the face in the mirror shows a measure of fulfillment that makes up for its lack of perfection.

Chapter 10

OFF TO EUROPE

The new year brought more challenges and opportunities, as described by Elizabeth in a January 1954 letter to good friends Gina and Alexander Brook. The Brooks were well-known artists who divided their time between New York and Savannah. Alex had painted portraits of both Elizabeth and Penelope.

> This is to thank you for your sweet Christmas greeting. Today is cold and grey despite a profusion of over eager camellias and daffodils; and as you requested, here is news of the Cokers. Christmas morning found us very gay with the third stocking at the mantle, that of the dear son-in-law. Little James was hilarious with a 'family,' and our day was a merry, old fashioned one with visits to and fro among the family.
>
> The next day, old gremlin started to work as a thick fog descended and Penelope and John driving back from a party in Darlington with young cousin Edgar Lawton had the misfortune to run into a mule who couldn't decide which side of the road had the greenest grass. All of a sudden there was a crash, and Penel looked straight into the wild-eyed face of a huge grey mule just as he leapt through the windshield and landed against her chest!
>
> Fortunately, she threw up both her hands so she had only a long cut on her neck, both wrists badly jagged, and a deep bruise on her chest. This rather quieted the rest of the Christmas which may have been a good thing for after having spent the fall standing on her feet for nine long hours a day for Hattie Carnegie's salon as the dark model, she [Penelope] needed the rest. John spent the rest of the time rather dazedly saying over and over in a low voice, "Oh to be back in the safe city

streets once more."

I am working on a new book, commuting back and forth to Charleston (a half-hour flight), delving into musty old books with a few sparkling moments on the side. Jim is taking James to New York to spend his 13th birthday with Penelope and John.

Penelope is having a fascinating time. She gave up her modeling job to do a TV program about shooting in South Carolina. She hates guns, but is excited about the new career. Jim and I are off soon on *The Liberte* for an International Congress of Industry meeting in Paris and Germany for a tour of manufacturing plants and to be entertained in high style. Jim has spent the winter devising a scheme to definitely break the bank at Monte Carlo, so we will have a splurge in Monaco.

Our love – Elizabeth

• • • • •

On April 23, 1954, the evening before Elizabeth and Jim departed for Europe, Penelope and her husband, John, hosted a *bon voyage* party in New York. Elizabeth lavished praise on her daughter: "Much proud of her poise and aplomb as well as the finesse of her decorations and food. After[wards], Jim and I, with the Ogden Nashes, saw Audrey Hepburn and Mel Ferrer in 'Ondine' [on Broadway], which – unlike most fantasies – was pure magic."

The next morning the Cokers boarded *The Liberte.* Elizabeth recounted the ensuing weeks in her diary as they crossed the Atlantic and toured Europe.

Saturday, April 24 – To embark on *The Liberte* around 10am amidst delightful confusion. Room full of flowers and people, including Penel and John and pretty Rivers girls [daughters of Martha and John Rivers of Charleston]. Boat (the old *Europa* built by Germans) smooth as a hotel. Attractive couples: the Bradfords from Nashville (they've been at my house in Blowing Rock) and the [H.] Mays from Burlington, N.C. We are going to have fun.

Sunday, April 25 – Sea calm as silver glass. Cocktails with Mays after dinner, dancing at the Cafe Atlantique. Captain Dublineau asked me to dance twice. He's youngish, tall, gay and pleasant. A good dancer, but not as good as J.C. Bradford.

Tuesday, April 27 – A heavy, heavy sea! Always to excite me and make me want to sing and move about. All ropes and guards up. Few people. Jim early to bed. I to stay and the captain did come and ask me to dance, and the Bradfords and I joined this group where we made merry till dawn.

Wednesday, April 28 – Awakened at 11:15 by the steward saying crossly, "Arise at once, Madame, the Captain expects you on the bridge at 11:45!" With much haste I arose and did partake of a lovely punch of rum and a slice of lime, while the Captain read me from a book of verses writ by him.

On to meet Jim and we lunch in a festive mood and walked on deck in a high wind, and later danced all night. Jim went to bed around 1:30 and looks quite peaceful. I am not peaceful but over excited and so, so terribly restless.

Thursday, April 29 – When the steward brought my breakfast, he brought a sealed envelope from the Captain. I quietly tore it open to find a poem he'd written last midnight while on the bridge. I fear it is not respectable from what I can read of it . . . later, much more alert now. It is after 3am and such wondrous dancing with J.C. Bradford and now it is an onerous duty to be charming to the Captain who do appear over eager.

Friday, April 30 – Into Havre around 5pm, train trip through Normandy to Paris was thrilling. So fair the face of France! How could the Huguenots have left their apple trees – their poplars – their snowy geese – the green fields for the wilderness of Carolina?

Saturday-Sunday, May 1-2 – Perfect Paris days. Walks around the Rue de la Paix and the Place Vendome, lunch at the Ritz, cocktails with the Bradfords, the Mays, etc. Jim and I very merry, then to Maxim's at 10, and after dinner to Monseigneur's in Monmarte. Charlie Babcock took up with one of the singers and gave me his bottle of nitroglycerine to hold "just in case." H. took up with a Spanish girl, Jim with Bibber May, and I with J.C. and his wife with a man at the next table; and I laughed more than I have laughed in 10 years.

Next day, I have to meet my father's cousin Sarah Watson at the Louvre. Sarah has lived in Paris for 40 years, is a tiny and broad little old woman with an exquisite face and a stern Alice B. Toklas like companion. She wore a hat of ostrich plumes that danced in the wind, and her leg was in a cast, but she could get along better than I despite.

Later, the directors of our English company flew in, so Jim and I joined them and our regular group for dinner at L'Escargot. I asked for *frais du bois* and the waiter couldn't understand so I said *frais sauvage* and he burst out laughing then fetched in great style a huge crystal bowl of the tiny luscious berries and great pots of thick cream.

Monday, May 3 – Jim and I went to Gres [French haute couture fashion house founded by Madame Gres, aka Alix Barton] and selected a dress of pale blue lace, and I arranged to come back for a "body" fitting at 4:30. Lunch and a walk in the Tuileries, then back to Gres to be ushered into a small room with three chairs before three long mirrors. In one sat a German lady with flax hair (the daughter of the Kaiser, married to Don Jaime, the deaf mute heir to the throne of Spain) stark naked; and in the other, reading a magazine, wearing a brassiere only, the Duchess de Rochefaucald. She could have been anywhere between 40 – 60, so beautifully cared for was she. "Take it off," said my sales lady (Madame Eva). So, thinking if royalty can, I can, I did! And Madame Eva shrieked "Une blonde naturelle!" And the Duchess lifted her lorgnette and looked and the Princess (who should have been and wasn't) stared, and two little models peeped through a curtain, and I wanted somebody to wink at, but there being nobody just stood and waited nonchalantly for "my body."

Tuesday, May 4 – Beautiful train ride to Venice, waking in Milan. How different the trip than the one in 1935. No customs to bang on the door at 3am, no soldier to burst in and push my feet off the seat with his rifle stock – no soldiers everywhere – everywhere – no Mussolini anywhere. To arrive in Venice and find it all true! The one place even more so that even I could imagine. And so by water to the Royal Daniele . . . and later, immersed in Veronese and Tiepolo and wonderful food and wanderings through the most gigantically gorgeous rooms in the world. What people these Venetians were with their large conceptions. And so to Florence where we met old friends and were very gay . . . more beautiful pictures at the Uffizi than I have ever seen . . . and on to Rome.

Again we are with the Bradfords and the H. Mays who invited us to do the Vatican with them. An Irish priest, friend of H's took us about, and on our tour he pointed out a house where, he said, Mr. Mulligan lived before he became famous. And who is Mr. Mulligan? "Mr. Mulligan! You mean you never heard of Mr. Mulligan? The man who did so much for Italy then made the mistake of betting on Mr. Hitler?" Of course I knew. I said I wondered why his name was never mentioned and twenty years ago when we were here that his was the only name spoken and HE was Italy then. In Venice and Florence whenever I'd mention Mussolini, the guide would shut up like a clam. "No," said Father Doyle, "his name is never spoken in Italy." Someday when the violence and bloodshed for which he is responsible, the suffering and the disappointment in their leader is forgotten –

. . . We ended up by visiting the Egyptian wing in the Vatican and by now, being weary, I made a few caustic comments about the resemblances of certain statues, and Father Doyle sternly reprimanded me and threatened to lock me in the mummy room until midnight. I said all right, provided he'd come back for me and he said I was no Christian child.

Then he challenged me to race him down a long flight of marble steps and I did. He flew down ahead of me, his robes billowing about like graceful black bird wings – laughing back at me. What a darling . . . after lunch at Tres Scalini we got back into H's limousine and drove out along the Appian Way through the half-finished marble city Mr. Mulligan had started in his honor as a world's fair to begin with, and then to have become the center of government. A terrific dream. What a pity he backed the wrong horse. Tomorrow is my father's birthday. May 11.

Wednesday, May 12 – Wandered the city all morning, and after lunch at Capricio, we prepared for our tea at the Palazza Sermonetta with the Duchess, who was a Colonna and married a Caetani – uniting two of the oldest most noble Roman families. Naturally we'd hired a limousine and a driver. I wore my chartreuse Nettie Rosenstein and freshly new white kid gloves and when we told the Concierge at the Excelsior where to tell our driver to take us, he paled with reverence and almost bowed to the ground as he helped me into the car.

The Palazza was on a hill near the Forum. There were marble bears on the gateposts, and at the entrance a long flight of red velvet covered marble steps with a clean white linen strip about a yard wide placed on the center. Suppressing a nervous giggle, I nudged Jim and with much dignity we ascended to barred crystal doors which a man in impeccable livery opened. "The Cokers," I said haughtily, and he indicated that we were to follow him; which we did through wondrous dim-ceilinged and wall-decorated mystic rooms into a paneled room where burned a cheery fire and where sat two perfectly beautiful, tall, carefully coiffed ladies – the Duchess (looking a well cared for 65) and her sister the Marchessa (at least 85).

"Tea immediately," said the Duchess and then – "Of course, I'm quite an ill woman. I am in the very center of a nervous breakdown. Do you take cream? Mrs. Coker, will you pass the sandwiches?" We talked world affairs and when she asked where we were going next, I said Monte Carlo and Jim explained his "system" to her and she told him what her husband's system has been and everything was much at ease. The Duchess announced that as she found us charming and could breathe quite well since our arrival, she would show us the palace. She had not done a showing since the Queen of England's and the Duke's visit last and she hoped we had more appreciation of it than they did.

She towered over me making me feel like a low legged fuzzy blonde kitten. But the minute we were in the next long gilded salon, I saw in a cabinet a pair of Ming wrestlers in white porcelain. Never having seen figures like these and utterly entranced, I stopped and almost shouted, "Look at those gorgeous Ming men!" The Duchess beamed. "So interesting that you would notice. Few do." She said that they were the only ones of their kind known; then she showed me a box of Saxe china, a tea set that Queen Victoria had given her granny. "Never found an occasion grand enough to use it."

We passed from room to room coming finally to an octagonal marble room in the center of which was a pedestal and on it the marble head of a beautiful woman. "The first Caetani done by Phidas in the 6th century B.C." I made appreciative comments and the Duchess continued: "What a relief you are. Queen Elizabeth and the Duke merely looked at the head and Elizabeth said, 'Rather resembles the Duchess of Kent, eh what?' They know nothing of art." At last, we excused ourselves and walked with aplomb down the long white marble steps to our car.

We dined with the Bradfords at La Palazza, the former nest of La Belle Petacci [Clara Petacci] – Mussolini's mistress – where Mr. M came at day's end to relax and make love; and here, so say the Italians, he lost his integrity and became soft. We had one of the best meals I've had anywhere, and afterwards we drove to the Colosseum in the black and silver moonlit night. Such a feeling of man's permanence was there that night in the moonlight with this colossal dream still distinguishable about us. It was good to have Jim and the Bradfords to share it with. Oh dear. Our last night in Rome. What a perfect day. I think one of the most enjoyable I've ever known.

Thursday, May 13 – Flew low over Elba and thought of the hopelessness of an eagle [Napoleon Bonaparte, who was exiled here in 1814] being grounded there. Landed in Nice and were driven to Monte Carlo. Monte appeared bare and deserted. Our driver Mr. Lassa says the opening of the Casino at Nice and the one at Mentone have completed the ruin of the place. The people who kept the place going in olden days are gone. The English can't bring enough money out of England and the Russian aristocracy is nonexistent.

Walked in the gorgeous garden of the Hotel de Paris, and that night to the casino. Evening clothes are no longer a "must" and what a change in the customers. Of course there are still a number of raddled old women with their pretty boys in attendance, but no wicked or smooth looking gentlemen. I chatted with the croupiers and did a spot of desultory gambling, but it genuinely bores me, so why bother? Jim stayed on, loving it. I heard him come in before dawn. He was humming and did a few dance steps en route to the loo. He must have won a pile. I snuggled happily in my soft down pillows.

The next day we walked, had a marvelous lunch at Oscar's, then to the aquarium. I don't like fish. They repel me. I'll probably be eaten by one someday. Jim is fascinated by them. To the casino again and Jim went merrily about his game doing his "system." All of a sudden I decided what the heck, so bought some fat stakes and plunked them all down on number 20 thinking surely it was my winner but no, no – all was raked away on the turn of the wheel so I told Jim "Good night" and meandered back to the hotel. Our room looks out over the sea. Tonight is very beautiful and still. There is a mist low and the jaggy shore seems soft and gentle. I do hope Jim is winning and the pretty lady he has "taken up" with is worth it.

Saturday, May 15 – To Germany. The train trip up the Rhine unbelievably enchanting and so long as we follow the Rhine. The beauty continued, but on reaching Cologne the desolation began. From there on to Essen is a nightmare of destruction. My first experience with bomb damage. Oh, I'd seen London in 1950 hit by fire and bombs, but that was compassed in terms of blocks – this went on for miles. I was exhausted and frightened by the time we reached Essen; itself a black skeleton of a town – the moon shining like a jack-o-lantern ghoulishly through the torn and twisted buildings. No majesty in these ruins as in the Colosseum seen by moonlight! At the Essener Hof, an old-fashioned room with a bed covered by a square eiderdown sewed up in a white sheet. All night burning up under it and freezing when pushed it back. I should not have come here. Jim says it will look different in daylight.

Sunday May, 16 – Joined our group for lunch at a lovely restaurant overlooking the Ruhr Valley. There are some attractive couples in the group, and indeed things are looking better in daylight. I think we will enjoy the week. This afternoon were driven about the huge Krupp empire. No birds sing here. Almost half of the machines were dismantled under disarmament for Germany. The Krupp fortune was destroyed and Alfred Krupp imprisoned. In 1950 new manufacturing firms settled in the Krupp area. There were 60,000 industrial workers before the war; 18,000 now.

Tonight, the grapevine got the message to us Americans to dress up. I wore my champagne lace, sure that I would shine brightly only to be greeted by Mme. Fritz Berg, wife of the president of the German Federation of Industries. She stood in the door wearing Christian Dior's most exquisite creation – a brown silk organza ball gown with wreaths of intricate white silk roses embroidered over the huge skirt. Feeling a bit dowdy, I walked on into the lounge of the Essener Hof. The German ladies had really made an effort to appear well and had on creations of great formality completely putting us Americans in the background.

During cocktail time, none of the Germans greeted us or spoke until we went in to dinner where there were always three or four Germans who spoke English at each table for eight. Husbands and wives were at separate tables. Jim was seated by Baron Krupp, who is starkly handsome in a thin sort of way. I was across the room beside Herr Hugo Stinnes whose family (steel, coal, shipping, etc.) before the war was the wealthiest in Germany. We spoke of the strangeness of our chatting together when nine years ago we were enemy to each other. Then he got to talking about the war and he told me how some of the American officers had occupied [his family's] *schloss* [palace] and behaved well, and that some others had abused his furniture and broke and destroyed the family heirlooms.

Then remembering that the purpose of this whole "do" was to impress on the American businessmen Germany's ability to run herself profitably and amiably, he turned the talk to our children. I was delighted. During his discourse, I opened my bag for a hankie and he having told me of his two little girls loving hair bows, and finding the festive captain's dinner ribbon from *The Liberte* with "Liberte" embroidered in gold on it, I impulsively took it out and said, "Here, give this to your little girls to play with." Whereupon he turned crimson and said – "Take it from my sight. That was my father's ship."

Oh, dear. After dinner, duty being done, the sheep and goats again separated and went into the lounge where coffee, French brandy and cigars were offered. When I left, I went over to Mme. Berg and thanked her for a lovely evening. She didn't even bother to rise, but said coolly, "Good night." And so to bed.

By May 20th, we are in Berlin. In East Germany there is only one street rebuilt: the *Stalinstrasse* [aka *Stalinallee*], made up of workers who live under piles of bricks. In the shops there are only two prices, one four times the other and only people with Communist party cards may purchase at the cheaper counter. "We are well fed," chanted a group that followed us. "We are well clothed. We have jobs. Go home and tell Mr. Dulles to make peace." The destruction everywhere is unbelievable. What a hell the war must have been here. Guards are everywhere.

And now Paris. The highlight of which was the evening in Versailles. Wore my white lace and long white gloves and looked rather well. Jim wore his top hat and no overcoat having lost it in Florence. Our group transported by grand buses arrived at about nine.

I've never seen so many ladies in such gorgeous ball gowns. Saw Harvey Firestone and many old friends and met people from all over the world. Our man Prentiss came in with the

President of France, and we were asked to sit on the terrace and listen to Charles Boyer read a history of the chateau by Andre Marois (accompanied by the Paris Symphony Orchestra). I saw it all as plain as if a thousand actors had been there.

The only drawback a freezing bitter wind. Jim wrapped his head up in Gladys Moore's shawl and I scrunched down little between Lew [Lewis Kleinhans] and Jim and asked them to break wind on either side of me. Lew thinks I am completely insane.

Later we were directed by footmen in white wigs and court livery, each holding high, gold candelabrum, up to the gold gallery where long tables loaded with the most beautiful food and champagne were presided over by resplendent serving men. I still can't take in the fact that I, Elizabeth, have been to a ball at Versailles given by the President of France and attended by so many grand ones. It's a long way from the Pee Dee swamp to the gold gallery.

By May 27th, many speeches and dinners and drinks of champagne and mad shopping; later, we have 13 pieces of luggage, and we are off to the Savoy in London . . . and now, back home. How wonderful it's all been and is. A most perfect adventure.

Chapter 11

JIM

Six months after returning from their glorious tour of Europe, the Cokers received distressing news, which Jim related in a letter to a friend.

> In January 1955, my world ended. At least that's what I thought when I was told late one afternoon in New York that I had cancer. That morning the doctor had taken a small piece of flesh out of the bottom of my mouth to have the laboratory perform a biopsy. He did not expect to have a report until the next day so I was going home that night. At six o'clock that night he called me at my hotel and said "I'm sorry, it's malignant. I want you to come by my office and let me consult with another doctor who will be here soon."
>
> I couldn't believe it, but I went back to his office. Another doctor looked at my mouth and felt inside and outside of it and they both agreed that surgery was necessary.
>
> "Couldn't I wait a month to take a trip my wife and I had planned?"
>
> "No, but you can go home and get ready to come back in a week." There was nothing else to do but agree, so I asked him to call my wife and explain it to her. When he got Elizabeth on the phone and told her, I could hear and feel the momentary silence at her end. But as usual, she was quick on the uptake.
>
> I got home the next morning and told the officers at the plant and some of my relatives what had to be done. Then I went to work and started to get all my personal business affairs in shape so that whether or not I come back, things could be carried out with no real interruption.

> Six days later Elizabeth and I took the train back to New York and I entered the hospital. I learned then that the first operation would be preparatory and the real one would come a week later. The preparatory operation was a gastrectomy and a tracheotomy – both of which seemed to me, when I woke up after they were performed, to be major ones.

On January 24, Elizabeth wrote their friends Martha and John Rivers of Charleston:

> So much appreciated your call. Jim and I are in a state of semi-shock I suppose and are forcing a semblance of normalcy into our days, which have put on a most tragic mask.
>
> Jim has a malignancy in his throat and under his tongue only discovered last Friday but already extensive. We leave for New York on Wednesday night – he goes into Presbyterian Hospital on Friday afternoon and the first operation will be on Monday. I will keep you informed. Our only prayer is – well – can't put it into words.
>
> But bless you for your friendship. Love, Liz

On February 3, Elizabeth penned this note, sent from New York, to her Aunt Reitta:

> Dear Reitta,
>
> Just a few lines to let you hear about Jim. He is in Presbyterian Hospital, Harkness Pavilion, to undergo an operation for a malignancy in his mouth and throat. He has passed the first operation successfully and will have the big one on Monday. The doctors are optimistic and so are we.
>
> I remember a passage in Pepys Diary [*Diary and Correspondence of Samuel Pepys, F.R.S.*] where Pepys goes to watch the

execution of the jury who condemned Charles I. Describing a certain Lord M – he says that while Lord M was being drawn and quartered he "exhibited as much cheerfulness as was possible under the circumstances."

Well – Jim and I are too. Much Love, Liza

On May 18, she wrote daughter Penelope.

Dear Penel, I am sitting on the Seaboard at Patrick [S.C.] in a car just run off the track!! A fitting occurrence in the nightmare of the past 24 hours. Da and I went to New York [on] Sunday. Monday, Dr. Hanford told him he wanted to keep him a week or ten days and heal up the open abscess in his throat. We decided I'd better come on home since James' recital is tomorrow night; and since Janie Wood [across the street neighbor and mother of Penelope's best friend, Mary Jane] had insisted on keeping him and since Edith does not like the Woods and since Edith is indispensable at the present.

On an impulse, I went to see Dr. Hanford by myself to be sure I should leave or could leave conscience free. He was in his office and said – What a coincidence. I was just getting ready to call you to come here. And then he let me have it – hard. They didn't get all the cancer out. There are two places left – one under his tongue; one under his jawbone. He must not be told. They plan to tell him the operation in July is purely restorative and hope to get the two places out then. However, I seem to have heard Dr. Hanford mention "possible removal of jawbone and/or tongue," but I couldn't bear to hear more. He plans to have another specialist see Da next week with him for advice. I agreed and so he said he'd tell Da he would let him come on home Thursday and back next week for observation and to meet Dr. Krimmen.

Somehow I have a feeling Da suspects. He has some mighty

blue moments. Oh dear I wish I knew what to say or do but I don't. I hated to leave him but if I'd changed he would instantly have suspected something. Now if the July job is not successful I think he should be told the whole story. He would know anyway. Poor soul – I can't believe he has been so wonderful and brave and all to no avail. Do write. He worries about you constantly. I hate to tell you this sad news but feel it is only fair. Don't refer to it when you write me. He might see the letter. I'll call you before long.

Dear, dear love, Ma

On June 19, she wrote another note to John Rivers.

Dear John – What a two weeks! Have never seen such suffering or such courage. Fortunately, the former is abating and the latter remains the same. Jim doesn't look too bad but it is not yet proven whether he can tolerate the wire jaw they shaped for him. If not, the young Chinese doctor will do a bone graft. They think they got it all.' If they did, I suppose life is worth it. If not – what a miserable waste. Martha [wife of John Rivers] never looked lovelier than when I saw her here. As always, your "girls" were sweet and wonderful to me. You are too. Bless you.

A few weeks later, Elizabeth sent a letter to Aunt Reitta, again from New York.

Dear Reitta,

I came back up here Sunday June 26 for four or five days in one medium suitcase and now have no idea when we'll get home. Last week was bad. But not all bad. The pathology report is in and proves ALL tumor is out! For that we are truly thankful, but will feel better when some of the current problems are solved! Our main and beloved doctor, Hanford, had a heart attack, and the doctor who was to take over in the emergency announced that he was leaving town. This despite the fact that an infection had set up around the wire mesh with which he had fastened Jim's jaw together and Jim running a high temperature. So all week we have been surgeon-less while a plastic surgeon and an antibiotic man had struggled with the abscesses. Needless to say, the pain and frustration have run neck and neck. Nobody would (or could probably) tell us anything definite. Just – we'll try this and try that and see!

Then last night in walked a young Chinese – Dr. Ju, looking to be about 20 but surely 30. The other doctors involved reviewed Jim's whole case for him. Still no satisfaction. A moonless night. But tonight Dr. Ju came in alone, sat down and in the most beautiful words in the world explained the whole situation to Jim. Condensed, it goes like this:

An infection has set in around the wire mesh. Dr. Meleney is trying by aspiration and Bacitracin to control this infection. Dr. Ju feels there is about a 25 percent chance of this. No more. SO in a few days if the infection is not responding, he will go in and take out the wire support. Then in three to six months, Dr. Ju will do a bone graft and GOOD restorative work. He also discovered Jim can't swallow except by gravity – (throwing a whole glass of stuff down at a gulp). Finally suggested X-ray on the saliva glands to dry up the constant drooling. The price for this will be a permanently dry mouth. All the time he talked I was conscious of a sudden mystical bond of confidence and affection between him and Jim. He was like sweet oil on troubled waters.

That then is the picture. At the end of a few days more, either the miracle drugs ARE a miracle or another anesthetic and the wire mesh out and at least ten more days in hospital. A minimum of two more weeks I fear. But then Jim will be well and able to go about his life again in a normal routine. It is

a long road but somewhere along the way courage is given.
Love, Liza

[P.S.] It's hotter than the hinges here. Oh – I do so want this to get over – Give Louise my love

• • • • •

Toward the end of the summer, in an undated letter to Hartsville neighbor Arabel Rogers, Elizabeth wrote:

Dear Arabella,

Yesterday Jim was desperate. Fever over 104 and in agony: whole area around the wire a conflagration of infection. Stood by for hours watching – watching; for now they daren't go in and take out mesh until fever abates somewhat.

I'm crazy about the young Chinese. He went to work and ordered old fashioned remedies [such] as alcohol sponges and wet packs after incising the chin to let pus begin to drain. Cutting out most of the antibiotics for fear he has had too much of them. This A.M. he [Jim] seems better but still very ill. Dr. Ju thinks he can go in by Tuesday and take out the wire. This will wreck the appearance of the jaw but he thinks will bring instant (relatively speaking) relief. Four general anesthetics. Came packed for three days to a week. May have to stay a month!! All depending on whether abscesses due to wire mesh quiet down or continue to flare. They don't want to do the bone graft under 4 more weeks; so if irradiation continues, he must stay here for daily care under Dr. Meleney, father of antibiotics. Young Charlie is here. Sailing tomorrow. Wish Joe were in the gay group. Life too full of hard things to miss the fleeting merriment.

Love Liz

And in another note to Arabel:

> Dear Arabella,
>
> Sitting here listening to the chimes of St. Thomas [Episcopal church near St. Regis Hotel in midtown Manhattan] across the street. They are saying "There is a wideness in God's mercy – " Last night I had supper with my agent. She's English – my age – nice, cozy husband she supports. She has been wonderful to Jim. Goes up 2 to 3 times a week and reads to him. She said (last night) "What a tremendous change in Jim. From a shy, rather silent introvert – he is becoming an outgoing extrovert. He talks so much more – so interested in other people – so many things!" Maybe that's the "wideness" in his care. He can suddenly share himself. So unlocked from the cage of staying inside. Wants to share –

• • • • •

Twelve months passed. On September 13, 1956 – back home at Loblolly Hill in Hartsville – Elizabeth penned this poignant message to Aunt Reitta:

> Dear Reitta,
>
> A summer of becoming adjusted to the limitations – which now are beginning to prove that no matter how much Jim tries he has reached his maximum plateau of recovery – is about past. It was easier to take the big blows last summer than these continuous small disappointments. However, the malignancy is cured (a word which I use *arriere pensee*), and he continues to take speech lessons from a precious little German-Jewish refugee at Mt. Sinai Hospital whenever he is in New York.
>
> We spent two separate weeks at Blowing Rock and the climate was perfect for him and soothing to me. But I must say that I can work better here in my stifling hot little cubbyhole amid

piles of dusty books, papers, cockroaches and mice than on top of the world with nothing to break the cool silence except a screech owl on a maple tree outside my window, and an occasional wood thrush sounding miles away down the gorge – but really in my front garden on a prize Comanche dahlia.

• • • • •

For several years Jim prevailed, steadily and bravely. He grew a beard to hide the disfigurement from the many throat and mouth surgeries. Against the odds, he adapted and managed to speak coherently again – far better than any of the doctors thought possible.

Under Jim's leadership, Sonoco Products Company had become a global leader in the manufacture of packaging materials – increasing in size and scope by a factor of 20, extending its branches into nine other states and four foreign countries, and greatly diversifying its product line. Jim served as president of the Bank of Hartsville and president emeritus of the board of trustees of Coker College. He was also a director of the National Association of Manufacturers, the North Carolina National Bank, the Carolina Power and Light Company and several Sonoco affiliates in the United States and abroad.

Jim won countless awards for his philanthropy, vision and hard work. Despite growing physical discomfort due to his cancer, he continued to find joy in his travels, speaking engagements, and above all, his family. He was particularly proud of Elizabeth's career as a writer.

Then in early 1961 Jim learned that his cancer had returned. After a brief period of additional surgery and curative measures at New York's Presbyterian Hospital, he succumbed to the disease on February 16 at the age of 56.

In a March 4 letter to Jim's dearest friend, Mac McKenna of New York, Elizabeth wrote the following:

> Most beloved Mac,
>
> Strange that you were not there at the end. Yet I would not have wished it for you. You, who were there at the beginning when there was so much hope; you, who came from Wall

Street through the miles to 168th Street, day after day, month after month, to his room where we laughed and we all kept our flags high because we were so sure man did have a chance. Jacob wrestled with the angel. We thought often of Jacob who came away from his dark battle with a limp. We thought, too, of Job who in the end, after all the years of tribulation and lamentation, triumphed.

We did not envision the end that really came to be. I remembered three years ago – it was September, no, it was early October and it was just after Jim had a spell coming home from Hot Springs – I followed you down from our apartment in the St. Regis to the street in New York and you said to me, "I know just how you feel for I buried my father so many times before he died."

The past three years I have alternately buried Jim and celebrated festivals with Jim. Depth and heights; fears and rejoicing; gloom and gaiety; always tenderness, devotion, humility, courage – always the flag high.

I can't say though there were times during the time when I would have given my soul for your arm around me, that I wished you were there to share the descending flag, the sudden spoken word, "Man has no chance against the Dark Angel." You cannot imagine the fight Jim Coker put up. There was one few-minute interval – my brother and I in the room with him, just after the doctor told him the biopsy was suspicious and X-ray expedient – when he cried a moment and said, "They say this is it."

After that no more words except mundane words and a possession of him by a burning fever (from the advanced stage of the disease, which he was in so suddenly that it was almost from one day to the next). Then there was the true wrestling with the Dark Angel; the dreams; the attempts to flee the hospital.

"Go and get my clothes," he would order loudly. "I have an appointment downtown at the Bank that I cannot afford to miss. Go and call my lawyer. I must see him. Tell him I am taking a cab to his office at once. I don't like this hotel room. Something evil is lurking in the closet. You know I've got to get away. You must come with me. McKenna is outside in the hall. I told him I would come. Why won't you bring me my shoes? Charlie Campbell is in the hall. He's been out there all night. John Martin is behind the screen and so is that other person."

Friday night, before Jim died on Thursday, James came up from Chapel Hill. Jim said, "Now you can fire all the orderlies and the nurses. I want my son to do everything for me." Oh so tenderly, James changed Jim's pajamas; took him in his arms like a baby to the bathroom; sat by him, loved him. On Saturday Jim was in, what they now tell me, the state many people achieve during a 24-hour period of the week before death – a euphoria. It was a gala. We told jokes, we were merry. It was the strangest festival you can imagine.

That night, James left early to take Kathy [McKenna] to dinner and to see Olivier in "Becket." I stayed on and Jim's wild mood changed from gaiety to restlessness, before I left about ten o'clock.

At midnight, the night nurse came on; at 12:20 she went to get Jim a hypodermic; at 12:30 she came back in the room, but he had disappeared. Nobody in Harkness [Pavilion] had seen him go up one hall or down another. Searches were made; closets opened (bear in mind that he had been too weak for days from the fever to even walk to the bathroom); an overall alarm of Presbyterian Hospital sounded.

And where was Jim Coker? He was down on snow-packed Broadway, barefoot, in his pajamas, having opened a door out from the sunporch – so heavy it took two ordinary people to open it – and climbed down ten flights (we were on the tenth floor of Presbyterian) on the ice-coated iron fire escape in the bitter night (it was below zero and a hard wind blowing).

A policeman found him huddled in a snow bank calling for a taxi to take him home to South Carolina. The policeman rushed him to the emergency room at Presbyterian. An alarm had been sounded and the whole hospital staff was looking for him. There was not a mark of an injury on him. Not a bruise. Not a scratch. Nothing frozen – not even his fingers. He caught no cold. His wonderful 80-year old surgeon had no difficulty explaining the miracle: "The Angels bore him on their wings."

The next two days Jim continued to struggle to get away from SOMETHING. It wasn't that he didn't know who we were; [he could] carry on a conversation. It was just he must elude, he must escape, he must keep fighting. Thursday morning when I arrived at the hospital the nurse said, "He's taken a sudden turn for the worse. He would have gone an hour ago but he was waiting for you to get here." I ran over to the bed. His eyes caught mine. He grabbed my arm with a grip strong enough to have broken my wrist. Connection was made. Spiritual and physical. I was there. He gave a long down-going sigh.

Have you ever seen El Greco's "Descent from the Cross?" It was that way. I stumbled over to the window and flung it up. It was snowing hard. The wind howled.

"Oh, Mrs. Coker, why are you opening the window?" The nurse ran and flung her arms around me, pulling me back. She must have thought I was going to jump. "To let his soul fly out of this room. To let him go."

I won't go into the desolate hours that followed. The wild

> "getting home." Floyd McGowin hired a little Bonanza and Penelope and I flew from Teeterboro [N.J.] to Florence [S.C.], arriving around 9pm. Jamesy was there to meet us, heartbroken, noble in grief, all of a sudden grown very tall; as always, kind and tender. Jim arrived home by train Saturday morning.
>
> Such a funeral could only be had in a small town or a small country when a hero has passed. Why, we even rode down Main Street on Saturday afternoon from the church to the cemetery, all the stores closed, the streets packed and lined with negroes and farm people and mill people and town people and it was truly a hero's farewell. There is nothing in the world like a small Southern town on a Saturday afternoon.
>
> I couldn't help thinking, "He's loving every minute of it." Dear Mac, I just wanted you to know how it was. How he always loved you and believed in you. You were his best friend.
>
> With love.

• • • • •

Condolence letters and tributes poured in. Nearly every newspaper in the state carried an editorial marking Jim's death. The *Florence Morning News* declared:

> By any measuring stick, James L. Coker III was one of industry's titans. The manufacturing enterprise which he headed was world-wide.
>
> Heir to the wisdom and management of his father, C.W. Coker, and his grandfather, Major James Lide Coker, he came to the head of the Sonoco Products Company when the country was in deep depression. Under his leadership, it has continually expanded until today it operates plants in this country from the Atlantic to the Pacific coasts, one in Mexico, and affiliates

in foreign countries.

Paralleling his success as a manufacturer has been the success which has attended his management-labor policies. These policies have resulted in one of the country's most conspicuous examples of enlightened management, and account for the inspiring loyalty existing between labor and management in the Sonoco Industries.

The measure of a man may be taken by how he combines a good heritage with his own native talents to carve his own place in the world.

James L. Coker III was conscious of a good heritage. He had talents of his own which reflected the wealth of that heritage. These he combined in a remarkably successful career. And in making a place for himself, he made life richer and fuller for all his associates and employees.

The News and Courier of Charleston offered this testimonial:

. . . The integrity, intelligence and human qualities for which the Coker family has been famous have been exemplified through industrial, agricultural, civic and educational fields. James L. Coker stepped with grace and dignity along the paths where duty took him.

When illness required a disfiguring operation, he did not retreat into solitary retirement. He grew a beard to hide the scars, and continued to administer the business and participate in civic and social affairs. His fortitude became a fresh source of admiration.

Mr. Coker's death at 56 is a grievous loss to our state and our country. *The News and Courier* joins with his friends and family, and with the community of Hartsville to which the

> Cokers have given so much, in mourning this kind and capable gentleman. His memory will be green among us.

Finally, *The Hartsville Messenger* concluded its tribute with the following lines by 18th century poet Alexander Pope:

> "Statesman, yet friend to truth! Of soul sincere, in action faithful, and in honor clear, who broke no promise, served no private end, who gain'd no title, and who lost no friend; ennobled by himself, by all approved, praised, wept, and honored."

Chapter 12

STORYTELLER NONPAREIL

Elizabeth wrote her first book, *Daughter of Strangers*, "in the closet and behind kitchen doors." After its publication, she realized that if she was to continue to take her literary career seriously, she needed a quiet, private place to write. She explained that while Penelope and James were young, "writing was never first in my life. I had to write when it suited. I had a husband and children to look after and they always came first."

On Christmas morning of 1950, a miniature Christmas tree appeared on the porch of a tiny cottage in the front garden of Loblolly Hill. Full of cultivars, wildflowers and vegetables, the garden was a haven for songbirds – birdwatching having become a favorite pastime of Elizabeth's. In earlier days, the little cottage had served as a pony stall, then a playhouse. Now it was Elizabeth's "writing house," thanks to Jim.

"[Jim] gave me a building just for spreading out papers and writer's mess," she recorded in her journal. "That's exactly what I needed, more than diamonds or sables . . . It is my personal ivory tower that friends enter only under specific invitation. I find a good light; a shelf holding *The Oxford Dictionary, Encyclopedia Britannica, Dictionary of American Biography, The Bible,* and the newest *World Atlas*; a soft chair, and a big typewriter essential."

Elizabeth possessed the two elements vital to a female novelist, as articulated by Virginia Woolf in her 1929 essay "A Room of One's Own:" "A woman must have money and a room of her own if she is to write fiction." In the essay Woolf relates the story of a woman out on a walk, whose thought process had "let its line down into the stream," allowing her mind and imagination to flow freely as she strolled. As the woman starts to think of an idea, a park guard interrupts her, enforcing a rule whereby women are not allowed to walk on the grass. Enduring the interruption and abiding by the rule, the woman loses her idea. Here Woolf illustrates the impact of social expectations for women. She also makes a clear statement regarding women's intellectual potential, suggesting the absence of female fiction is due to a lack of opportunity, rather than an absence of talent.

• • • • •

Despite the constant demands of family and community, Elizabeth led a disciplined literary life, finding time for writing no matter what. Between the years of 1950 and 1959, she published five novels. People asked how she did it. She responded thus:

> I write every day. I write as many hours a day as I can steal from housekeeping without being downright neglectful. I never start anything that I don't finish. It isn't always good and sometimes it lands in the wastebasket as soon as I've read it over – but to no end, I go. I read hundreds of books a year. I keep my eyes open everywhere I go for a face, a pair of hands, a funny incident, a rare flower, an unusually beautiful sunset that I may be able to use later in a book.
>
> I keep a file of things like: hair, eyes, mornings – and the mornings are divided into fog, rain, sunny, happy, sad. The evenings are in the same categories, and the noons. I have stars in my files, and mountains, horses, trees, flowers – when they bloom, what color they are, where they grow. I have the sea, a man's thumb that I saw on a bus one day, noses, expressions, the way the sun flickers into my workroom window through the dogwood branches outside, birds, dogs, food. My food file would make your mouth drool it's so enticing. I try to do something just a little better, a little stronger, a little different than any other writer who has gone before me.

Elizabeth capitalized on and benefitted from the seismic shift in women's status that had occurred during her lifetime. She enjoyed more independence than most Southern ladies her age, telling a reporter from *The Charlotte Observer*: "I believe in careers for women and I believe I exemplify that. My greatest belief is that we should all live up to our greatest potential."

"The main thing to realize," she elaborated, "is that we women are strange, earthy, mystical beings whose schemings have caused more change and progress in the world by our devious and velvet gloved machinations than all the hydrogen bombs, battering rams, and longbows put together. It is ever woman, not man, who has the restless desire to influence the world, and seeks her magic ways thus to do."

She attributed the growing importance of Southern writers in the mid-20th century to a greater emphasis on education in the South. She was determined to prove H.L. Mencken wrong when he accused her homeland of being a desert of the arts.

• • • • •

During Jim's illness, Elizabeth kept writing. She published two more books with E.P. Dutton – *The Big Drum* and *La Belle*. The story of real-life figure Simon Blake (apprentice to London architect Christopher Wren), *The Big Drum* was the result of "unremitting research." In 1957, reviewer Virginia Ravenel of the Charleston *News and Courier* gave a brief summary of the narrative and a description of the author's approach:

> Blake is sent to Barbados to construct a central meeting house. Later he goes to Charles Town, which is the scene of most of the action in the novel. The time is the 17th century and those famous South Carolinians, Arthur and Edward Middleton, play their part in the plot.
>
> With her usual thoroughness, the author spent several years preparing to write this book. The first step was a trip to England in 1955. Through Louis B. Wright, director of the Folger Library in Washington [and fellow South Carolinian], Elizabeth obtained a letter of introduction to the Keeper of the Books in the British Museum. In this manner, she had access to material not available to the general public.
>
> In 1956 the author of *The Big Drum* went to Barbados for further research. She is no stranger to the West Indies, and has been making trips there for several years.
>
> In talking about her book, Mrs. Coker remarked, "Since no

> one has written of the first settlement of Charles Town by way of Barbados, I decided to use this theme. It is doubly interesting because of the West Indian influence still noticeable in Charleston. Each time I go there I am struck again by the marked similarity between the manner of speech, food and architecture of these two places."

Homebound due to his illness, Jim and Elizabeth spent the evenings at Loblolly Hill, reading aloud to each other and researching subjects of interest with intense focus. One winter they studied everything they could find on the D'Este family, a ruling dynasty in northern Italy during the medieval and Renaissance periods. The next year they investigated the Civil War, which led to Elizabeth's fifth book, *La Belle.*

Published in 1959, *La Belle* was based on the life of a Columbia, S.C. woman named Marie Boozer – much admired for her charm and beauty, but not entirely accepted into polite society. After Columbia burns at the end of the Civil War, Boozer leaves with Sherman's Army for New York on February 20, 1865. The protagonist suffers disgrace and divorce, then departs for Europe on a steamship, where she meets and marries a French count, becoming European nobility.

In her "Author's Note" at the beginning of *La Belle*, Elizabeth states:

> The truth about Marie, as always with the lovely and the lost, has been so lacquered by gossip, legend and anecdote that it has been difficult to separate the real woman from the mythical one. Thus while seeking out the mirror view of her I could never fail to be influenced by the spell she cast. To this day, people in Columbia still speak of Marie and her mother with as much curiosity, envy, admiration and opprobrium as they do of the fiery General Sherman who once visited the city.

Elizabeth read all of the "gossips" of the period – including reminiscences and memoirs – then checked legal documents and searched old newspapers and contemporary records. She was able to authenticate Marie Boozer's arrival in New York through the roster of the Union League Club, whose secretary was the grandfather of a friend and had the original minutes of the club's proceedings. Elizabeth likened recreating Marie Boozer's story to assembling a jigsaw puzzle, gathering myriad bits of information and knitting them together into a cohesive narrative.

> My "real life" information about Marie has come from many and varied sources and people, not all of them reliable. To establish a frame for her, I have used, at the top of each chapter, a documented quote from daily newspapers, diaries, letters, memoirs, records, legal papers, and history books. In addition, Marie's adoption papers, Dave Boozer's will, and Marie's letter to Julian Selby follow the wording of the originals. All these tell of a beautiful and exciting woman who in her short life traveled an exceeding long road.
>
> The renowned Dr. Babcock, of the South Carolina State Hospital, is said to have remarked on returning home from a trip across Europe in the early nineteen hundreds, "I came on Marie's trail everywhere I went and am sore afraid that our little Columbia girl has been guilty of sinning in many languages."

Sometimes referred to as the *Gone with the Wind* of South Carolina, *La Belle* sold well on its release and enjoyed three reprint editions – the last of which, in 1978, resulted in 700,000 paperback copies produced by Bantam.

Elizabeth's books were lauded for their recreation of the South's retreating and fading days. Her novels often featured a bibliography – testament to her extensive research and study. She gained renown as a brilliant chronicler of Southern life, especially the period before, during and after the Civil War.

• • • • •

Following Jim's death in 1961, people wondered whether Elizabeth would continue to write books. Those doubts were quickly put to rest. S.C. Poet Laureate Archibald Rutledge remarked in a note of sympathy to Elizabeth, "I think you very <u>gallant</u> to begin a new novel; the subject is original and fascinating."

Soon after, Elizabeth submitted a short story to the International P.E.N. competition. It was called "The Wishing Bone" and won third place in the world and first place among American P.E.N. contestants. "A reminder of the potency of her talent," commented one reviewer.

In 1963 she released her sixth novel, *Lady Rich* – the story of Penelope Devereux, who served as a lady-in-waiting in the English royal court. Since Jim's death, Elizabeth had been zealously studying the Elizabethan period and the court and courtiers of the Queen Elizabeth I, returning to Great Britain to conduct extensive research. The story of the beautiful Penelope Devereux (1563-1607) – who was fluent in three languages and a gifted singer and dancer – took Elizabeth to the British Museum in London, the Folger Shakespeare Library in Washington, D.C., and the Huntington Library in Pasadena, California.

Elizabeth had a talent for choosing captivating stories and characters from real life. She thoroughly researched the history and context of the era in which her protagonists lived, fleshing out their worlds with concrete imagery and fact-based details. In *Lady Rich*, for example, court pageantry of the late 16th century was well documented, supplemented by historic information regarding the Irish uprising, commentary on the liaison between England and France, and references to young writers of the period such as Bacon, Spencer and Shakespeare.

Like so many of Elizabeth's heroines, Penelope Devereux did not lead an easy or predictable life. Despite the glamour of the English court and her rank as a daughter of the Earl of Essex, Penelope was forced by a cruel uncle to forego two marriages that would have suited her. Instead, she had to marry the wealthy and brutal Baron Robert Rich.

Penelope rebelled against this marriage and lived illicitly with her true love, Charles Blount, the Baron Mountjoy and Earl of Devonshire. She bore Mountjoy eight children before finally receiving a divorce from Baron Rich in 1605 and becoming Mountjoy's wife, in defiance of canon law. Although both were banished from the court, they are buried together in Westminster Abbey.

When Elizabeth finally sat down at the typewriter to tell the story of Penelope Devereux – using Penelope's maiden name rather than the surnames of her two husbands – it took only seven months before a new manuscript was on its way to the publishers. In less than one week after publication, *Lady*

Rich entered a second printing. Skillfully combining suspense and intrigue with one of the most unforgettable love stories in English history, the book was considered by many to be her finest since *Daughter of Strangers*.

In 1968, Elizabeth published her seventh book, entitled *The Bees* and set in South Carolina. At the core of the story is Alexander Bee, known as "Grand." Ninety years old and possessed by the ambition of a man half his age, Grand Bee is proud king of a family textile empire in the early 1900s. But he feels his power ebbing and views his two greedy sons as petty tyrants. As a result, he sets his sights on making grandson Aaron the new president of the Queen Bee mill. However, Aaron proves to be an unwilling heir, setting in motion a powerful and unpredictable drama. Like her earlier novel *The Day of the Peacock,* the story of the Bee family provides a window into an emerging New South – an agrarian society changing into an industrial one – with its associated upheaval, uncertainty and opportunity.

By this time, in addition to writing novels, Elizabeth was reviewing books and composing poetry for various newspapers, magazines and anthologies. She had become deeply engaged in the literary and cultural life of her day, corresponding with fellow authors and poets such as Somerset Maugham, Ogden Nash, Burke Davis, Jonathan Daniels and Inglis Fletcher. She encouraged new talent, was in great demand as a reader and speaker, lectured throughout the South, and taught seminars at several colleges and universities – including Converse, Columbia and Coker colleges, as well as Appalachian State University. A member of the venerable Poetry Society of South Carolina, she was the featured speaker for their April 1971 meeting held in Charleston.

• • • • •

Elliott Macrae and his company E.P. Dutton continued to publish Elizabeth's works. While the relationship wavered at times – largely due to Macrae's outsized ego – the publisher understood Elizabeth's enormous talent and audience appeal, evidenced in a letter he wrote after reading her latest submission: "I didn't breathe or swallow while it raced along. All the time I read this manuscript I kept remembering you are a storyteller, and I always was conscious that here was a pro in action."

Elizabeth's next historical novel – *Blood Red Roses,* published in 1977 – proved Macrae right once again. The title was drawn from the sea chantey,

"Blow Down, You Blood Red Roses, Blow Down," and the setting of Hilton Head Island inspired by the many summers Elizabeth spent at her Aunt Ethel's (sister of Reitta) house on the May River in Bluffton. Hilton Head was a short boat ride from Ethel's dock and accessible only by water until it was bridged in 1956. "[The island] was all mystery and charm and secrecy and high excitement," she wrote in her diary. "One could reach it if one knew the tides and the winds and the currents. There was no other way."

Ever the zealous researcher, Elizabeth consulted old maps and reference works about the island and visited repeatedly. Her principal characters – Angelica, Elsa and Beau – evolved out of historic figures living in the area during the Civil War. The novel follows their journey from a Virginia plantation to Hilton Head, and chronicles the Yankee occupation of the island during the Civil War. As one critic stated, Elizabeth's imagery was "graphic and always appropriate to the setting:"

> Angelica has "heron-like beauty." Elsa's "mouth opens and shuts like an oyster's valves." The reader hears the "slap of the sea against the side of the steamer, and lonely cries of terns and cormorants and gulls" . . . *Blood Red Roses* has the gripping family conflicts, loyalties, strong plot development and psychological penetration of her earlier books. But this one has new dimensions – sensitive responsiveness to nature and a stronger sense of place.

Dedicated to her dear friends Lucy and Jonathan Daniels of Hilton Head, *Blood Red Roses* was an immediate hit. Less than a year after its release, Bantam Books paid a record price for the paperback rights.

Elizabeth's ninth and final book, *The Grasshopper King,* was released in 1981 when she was 72 years old. A sequel to her bestselling *Blood Red Roses,* the novel was set in Mexico following the Civil War. It is a story of two Confederate exiles, Angelica and Beau Berrien, as they leave postbellum South Carolina and follow Matthew Fontaine Maury (the Confederate naval officer) to build a new life in Mexico. Beau develops a close relationship with Emperor Maximilian, while Angelica becomes a lady-in-waiting to Empress Carlota.

In 1864, Emperor Napoleon III had chosen the Austrian Archduke

Ferdinand Maximilian Joseph of Hapsburg to assume the Mexican throne as his figurehead, backed by Mexican conservatives and monarchists during the French occupation. Believing he had the support of the Mexican people, Maximilian accepted the post and arrived in the New World with his young wife Marie Charlotte (Carlota).

At first, the royal couple enjoyed an idyllic life. But after a few years, Mexico's populist president Benito Juarez – a former supreme court justice – asserted his leadership with the support of the United States in opposition to Maximilian. Napoleon III ordered the withdrawal of the French military and Maximilian was deposed. Despite national and international pleas for clemency – including an appeal by Carlota to Pope Pius IX – Juarez ordered Maximilian's execution by firing squad in June of 1867.

In *The Grasshopper King*, protagonists Angelica and Beau are drawn into the power struggle inflaming the Mexican empire in the 1860s – finding themselves on the wrong side as allies of a figurehead installed by a hostile foreign government. Angelica tries to protect Beau, who is brave but a fool. As she struggles to save her husband, she becomes a central figure in the intrigue and danger of Maximilian's brief regime.

Elizabeth began writing *The Grasshopper King* immediately after the publication of *Blood Red Roses*. As she was starting research for the sequel, she explained to *Island Packet* reporter Fran Smith her rationale: "[Angelica and Beau are] conquered at the end of *Roses* [having lost the Civil War], and they're not people to be conquered. I've got to move them to somewhere else and go on with the business of living. They may go to Brazil or Mexico or Texas. I don't know."

On the release of *The Grasshopper King,* writer Jack Leland of Charleston's *Evening Post* asked Elizabeth why she took Angelica and Beau to Mexico, instead of Sao Paolo, Brazil – where they had planned to go with other former Confederates fleeing the South. She responded: "I decided I was too old to go up the Amazon alone. Had I a partner to go with me, they [Angelica and Beau] would have gone to Sao Paolo. However, I know Mexico quite well and I speak the language."

Elizabeth's connection with Mexico began in 1935 when she started collecting books on the country and studying Mayan culture. After World War II, Jim established the first paper mill there and the couple traveled to the dedication of the plant. They visited Mexico many times after that. Following Jim's death, Elizabeth returned annually for a month-long stay – shooting game birds, visiting ancient ruins and collecting pre-Columbian artifacts.

One of the young Mexican lawyers representing Jim (and Sonoco Company) was Hugo Margain, who became a lifelong friend. When Margain was appointed Mexico's ambassador to the United States, Elizabeth's research revealed he was the grandson of a Virginia Confederate by the name of Morgan. Morgan followed Matthew Fontaine Maury to Mexico after the Civil War, married into the Mexican aristocracy, and changed his name to Margain.

"How could I not choose Mexico as the scene for my story?" she asked Jack Leland at the end of their interview.

Chapter 13

1964: YUCATAN AND ISTANBUL

Mexico not only provided the inspiration and setting for Elizabeth's final book, it also sustained her in the decades following Jim's death. In the introduction to her Yucatan travel diaries of the 1960s – written on the release of *The Grasshopper King* some 20 years later – the author explains her enduring interest in Central America:

> My husband and I first travelled to Mexico in the late 1940s. Impressed with the people and the potential, [in 1951] he built one of the first American paper mills in Santa Clara, about eight miles from Mexico City. At the baptismal fiesta to celebrate the starting up of the paper machines, Jim made a welcoming speech to the workers in Spanish. (I think he was the first American businessman to have shown this courtesy!)
>
> After the fiesta, we toured the little village in a mule cart with the parish priest. We fell in love with Mexico and visited it every year. Since Jim's death in 1961, I have spent my Novembers in Mexico, climbing around among most of the fascinating Mayan and Aztec ruins; and safariing in the jungles of Yucatan, Quintana Roo, British Honduras and Guatemala to study the bird and plant life, as well as the people and the history of the regions.
>
> Lately, less adventurous, I have spent my Mexican month at the Balboa Club on the Pacific coast of Sinaloa at Mazatlan [an important port city], among the birds and flowers and Mexican friends of that area.
>
> In *The Grasshopper King*, I feel that somehow I have captured not only Napoleon III's grand design of empire in 19th century Mexico, but also the spirits of the corn god, the flower god,

> the sun god, the plumed serpent, the god of blood, the crumbling churches built by the conquistadores, the colonial cities of Merida and Campeche, the great haciendas of Cuernavaca, the soaring volcanoes, and the wonderful "today" Mexicans it is my privilege to name *amigos.*

• • • • •

Elizabeth suffered bouts of loneliness and sickness in the first few years after Jim died. Widowed at age 51, she described her struggles in letters to daughter Penelope and son James.

> The past week has not been easy, I having to, for the first time, accept the fact that I, EBC, must live alone . . .

> My house is full of the loveliest camellias. I took a basketful to the cemetery . . . The rest of the week I've just laid down and gasped feebly for breath, weary of it all.

> I hope someday I will be a happy, well dressed, thin old lady. As usual, when I'm not happy, I'm round and whipped cream fat as a pig. I eat dozens of onion sandwiches nightly, plus my iced tea glass of one martini . . . I'm tired.

> Our positions are reversing themselves. I am the one in need of TLC now! It's a weird day full of foreboding, but I dunno what of . . .

> To say Thank You is so little in return for so much that being repetitive won't in any degree express the gratitude and love I feel for having had the good/bad luck to fall to my doom in your house!

> It's hard to believe years have gone by. You [Penelope] and James have gone far ahead and I feel happy about both of you. I have gone steadily backwards in all ways – physically,

> emotionally, etc. Of course, this horrible weakness does not help, but the last culture has come back negative, so that means the infection has been local, not systemic, so I should begin to recover pretty fast now . . .
>
> I dread leaving this safe bed now that I have grown accustomed to it, but I suppose fate decrees that I must return to [the] land of reality, which is spelled H_A_R_T_S_V_I_L_L_E. I never felt less belonging . . . I am rootless in my own home.

• • • • •

Travel provided a necessary balm and catalyst, and kept Elizabeth engaged with the world. She joined friends and family on expeditions south of the border and overseas, often as many as three or four trips a year.

For writers, artists and scholars of the mid-20th century, Mexico represented a cultural and natural frontier, one that had yet to be fully explored by its neighbors to the north. Mexico also expanded Elizabeth's view of what it meant to be an American – a reprieve from the norms and expectations of small-town life in South Carolina.

Elizabeth's observations of the people and environment – set against the ancient backdrop of Mayan and Aztec civilizations, and the overlay of Spanish colonialism – were astute. She kept detailed and entertaining travel diaries, beginning with a tour of the Yucatan in January of 1964. Elizabeth and her friends arrived there on a brilliant sunny day, having boarded a jet from New Orleans in the middle of an ice storm.

> Wednesday, January 9 – . . . The drive into the city [the old colonial town of Merida, now the state capital of Yucatan] over flat land, spread out and exposed, into the beautiful old world Spanish "white city:" streets of exciting 17th, 18th and 19th century stone and stucco townhouses painted in pastel colors – lilac and blue and pink and cream and grey and green – all with long windows covered in intricate hand-wrought iron grilles; gorgeous blossoming vines a riot over the high walls; stone paved streets full of barefoot Indian women and girl children

> in white *huipils* (moo-moos!) brightly embroidered in red and green and pink and orange and blue flowers; Indian men and boys in white cotton blouses and trousers; Mexicans in white blouses and trousers and sandals swarming up and down, up and down; tiny horses pulling quaint little, gay painted buggy "taxis." Squares with dark green trees and stone benches and people at intervals; vintage cars blowing their horns at every corner; vultures everywhere – on the roofs, on the palm trees, on the street lamps. Every now and then a door is open and one sees through into a spacious cool green courtyard, surrounded by an arcaded gallery; one hears a fountain splashing and a macaw or a parrot screaming.
>
> The Pan Americana Hotel loomed up. O dear – a trap – a dump. But no – once inside the shabby Victorian cracked marble floored foyer, I followed the bellboy into the fountain court of an ancient and vast colonnaded Governor's Palace where four naked Venuses kneel around the blue marble pool and hold a lovely high spout of sparkling water. And, rearing behind the court, the shining new hotel, bug and heat proof!

That afternoon the group motored to the seaport of Progressa, where residents of Merida "progressed" during the hot months of the Mexican summer. Elizabeth described the road as "one goose-colored, frail road crossing the vast fields of sisal," and expounded in her journal about Yucatan's principal cash crops, the Sunday market in Merida, and the weather.

> Sisal is named for the Indian village on the sea where the Spanish first put in on this coast. It resembles a large century plant with tall straight spikey leaves from which rope and binder twine are made. (Looks and feels like our yuccas.) The other main source of income in Yucatan is the Sapodilla or Chicle tree from which chewing gum is made. But sisal is the crop of Yucatan on which the great hacienda-plantation system was built.

It was an afternoon all cloud and blue and big wind. On the way, we visited our first Mayan *ruinas*, which were off the main road in the middle of a sisal field: Dzabuitlin, from 200 B.C. It was just a few hot high piles of stone. We were not impressed. At Progressa, we stopped and had fresh coconut at a windy restaurant by the blue, blue sea. A big American came up and said sadly he had been here a week waiting to shoot ducks and that his vacation ended on the morrow. Would the wind ever change? We said, have a coconut and he said no, he'd go and look at the sky to see if the wind was changing.

Sunday, January 13 – On Sunday morning we went to the Market. It was teeming with Indian and Mexican farmers and vendors of every sort. A spread sack became a booth that held oranges, limes, eggs, tomatoes, radishes, chili peppers, carrots, bananas. There was the big fish market where we slipped on entrails and gagged on smells; there was the venison place where various parts of deer were sold; turkeys and chickens – long and raw and yellow-skinned – hung by their heads; hares by their legs. Old shawled women squatted about and offered tortillas and chicles and buckeyes (for the "stones") and sisal hammocks and sandals and cardinals in cages and yellow birds in cages and embroidered *huipils* [traditional tunic-like dress, often embroidered] and lovely lettuce. There were rows and rows of booths of sisal hats and handbags and mats. Buzzards flapped back and forth, back and forth.

That afternoon the rain. Poor American duck shooter! It blew and rained and blew and rained. Our round, low, pretty barefoot maid came in and I tried out my few Spanish words telling her who I was and about Penel and James. She smiled and nodded. I knew she understood not one word. We had early daiquiris in the bar by the swimming pool and a supper of little small pompano (*pampellita*) baked in banana leaves hot-seasoned with chile and tomatoes and grand crusty hot rolls that the waiter called *pan francia*. All night the big wind

> blew, the iron bells clanged and the roosters crowed and my stomach burned. At 8am I ordered *pan francia* for breakfast with my coffee and the waiter brought me cold squares of a seedy cake. He speaks pretty good English and I pleaded for the right word to get the supper rolls for breakfast. He told me; I said it after him.

• • • • •

Next on the itinerary was the World Heritage site of Uxmal – the ancient Mayan city containing some of the finest pre-Columbian structures in Latin America. The drive south from Merida captivated Elizabeth.

> Monday, January 14 – To Uxmal (pronounced Ooshmal): 35 miles of endless fields of sisal and primitive Indian villages. The round, one-room huts of the Indians are of stone, plastered over and roofed in palm thatch. Their only furniture is a table. They sleep in sisal hammocks which they hang back on a hook in the day. There are many thin cur dogs and an occasional donkey and lots of skinny chickens and half-clad children. Each village has a Square with a tremendous stone church with beautifully austere Spanish arches and towers. All crumbling and in disrepair, they are from the 16th and 17th centuries, but still in use. Every Square has a main market and rickety vegetable and fruit booths painted red and white with *Coca Cola Mas Grande, Coca Cola Mucho Mas* on them or *Pepsi Cola Mucho Mas.* There is usually a tall, pastel-painted clock tower in the center of the Square. Reminds [me] of the Barbados.
>
> Each village formerly belonged to a hacienda or a Spanish *grandee* [nobleman]. Now the anciently impressive wrought iron and stone gateways and the open factories – still making rope – are all that remain of that fabulously rich way of life. In Juarez's revolution, the Indians rose up and came and murdered and burned the owners that had not fled into Merida. The

government has taken away most of the rest. The descendants of the Spanish grandees are the ones who now live in the pretty houses in Merida (formerly their town palaces) in seclusion. Sort of like Charleston Lowcountry planters after Sherman and the New Deal did <u>them</u> in. Another sad fruit of Juarez's revolution was the great loss of Maya antiquary treasures and the burning of rare books printed by the early Franciscans – including a Mayan-Spanish vocabulary following Juarez's suppression of the religious orders.

The Hacienda Uxmal is a new, vast, galleried Spanish-type inn built around an extensive tropical garden and a long blue swimming pool. Big airy rooms. Ours looked out on a spectacular crimson flowering African tulip tree and undulant miles of palms and bananas and sisal; this afternoon shrouded in a chill mist, the wind having changed to the north. Vultures hung about the garden and atop the colonnade like gigantic black bees – jostling, shoving, parrying, leaping into the air, dropping. The beds were good, but the pillows felt as if they were stuffed with sisal spikes.

We decided it being only two [2pm], we'd walk over and inspect the ruins. Our pretty American landlady said a guide and a party were ready and we could join them. "You need a guide the first time," she said. "It's all so different." So [we] put on our sneakers and safari cloth trousers and off we trudged down the road and across a thicket and right bang up onto the Temple of the Dwarf – rising, like a man-made volcano from the ground. Its very steep stone stairway on either side must be climbed on all fours. How the gorgeous feather-clad bodies of victims, their living hearts ripped out, must have hurtled down them to the waiting Mayas below!

I had tried to read up on the Mayan civilization. I had a notion I would then be able to describe the feelings I encountered on seeing the ruins of it; but of course, I can't. I don't think

I have been more excited over anything. Not reverent Rome, not the ancient charm of Paris, not the violently beautiful coast of Wales . . .

As we entered the stone city I inquired of our Mexican guide as to the significance of a clump of finely carved toadstools, each about a yard high. "Those are phallic symbols," he said. "The Mayas were very worshipful of fertility. These were gathered here and there among *las ruinas*." I said, "Oh," and we went on about the various temples . . .

The loose grouped ruins [of Uxmal] have been partially restored by the Mexican government. This beautiful Puuc city, abandoned in 1000 A.D., is of the classical era. With all their skill, the Maya never learned the secret of the wheel nor the principle of the true arch; but used instead corbeled vaults, such as are found in ancient tombs of Greece and Italy. But the great wooden beams rotted and the roofs caved in and the buildings became a solid mass of stone and rubble which has had to be removed, almost [all] by hand. We visited the Governor's Palace – more than 300 feet of carved stone – room after room faced with undulating lines of masks of rain gods imposed on bold *grecques* [ornamental bands] and lattice work; and with writhing rattlesnakes complete with rattles to complicate the design. (And the Spanish came 4,000 miles to teach the Maya baroque!)

The Priests platform in front of the Palace with the two-headed jaguar, a head at each end, one head lower than the other, symbolizing man and woman. Between that and the Palace is a gigantic stone column plunging into the earth. I queried our guide. "Once again," he intoned, "a phallic symbol – the penis of the rain god fertilizing the good earth." There were many other "once agains" beautifully carved and attached to the buildings. There was the Temple of the Doves – a long facade of three triangles of latticed carved stone resembling a dove cote. No one knows what it WAS.

The Nunnery – the most spectacular of all the classically carved buildings – called by the Spaniards the Nunnery because of its quadrangle shape. The Temple of the Turtles, a gem of a building confined to engaged columns in the upper facade and a line of well-spaced realistic turtles on the upper cornice. Its austerity in direct contrast to the Governor's Palace exuberance. Swallows flew in and out of the windowless dark rooms. Snakes and "once agains" were carved everywhere. We walked up and down. It was very cold and grey. Sombre. No identifying of <u>me</u> with anything. In no other life have I ever been a Mayan. <u>No</u> familiarity . . .

Tuesday, January 15 – A brilliant sun. Guideless, we strolled the ruins. I lay on the grass terrace of the Governor's Palace and went to sleep, letting the sun's rays soak strength into me "once again." This should be all description – I mean of the green hills all around, each holding an undug temple; and the dark tropical garden of the inn; the big boat-billed flycatcher a whirl of gold, wings a fan of greeny gold, poised in air, eating an orange papaya fruit hanging over the blue, blue pool; the lush banana trees and flame crown of the African tulip tree; the Indian boys making the lovely pottery that the landlady designs; the round faced giggling little Indian maids in brightly embroidered white *huipils* (the same garment worn by the Mayan women in 600 B.C.!); the clouds of social flycatchers, like a gold net against the azure sky; the Indian *tocador* singing on the patio – sad Mexican songs like *Solamente Una Vez* and *Flores Negras*; and the ruins, over and over, the last day especially lovely – a pale blue, washed very sharp and soft on the sky – temple after temple. And that night I drank too much rum and was greatly upset, for which God forgave me.

• • • • •

On Thursday, January 17, the group rested for a day in Merida and then set out for Chichen Itza, the Mayan city built a millennium ago on the tip of the Yucatan peninsula. They checked in to Hotel Maya Land – an old stucco building with little stone huts clustered within a compound of tropical forest. Each hut had a thatched roof and two rooms filled with massive, indigenous designed furniture. Elizabeth absorbed every detail.

> We arrived about one [1pm] and an Indian boy fetched us lovely daiquiris. There were thousands of birds singing and calling. For lunch we had *arroz con pollo* (chicken and rice) and *frijoles* (mashed black beans) and *tortillas* (fried thin corn cakes). The best meal so far. After lunch we walked around and looked at the caged birds – they have several giant black curassows, the *faison real*, lots of ducks and assorted doves, and a few ocellated turkeys with their colorful glossy peacocky plumage.
>
> Then we drifted downroad to *las ruinas*. Being old hands by now, we bought a guide book. And this time we really didn't need a guide. Chichen Itza is infinitely better restored than Uxmal. The Carnegie Foundation has done a magnificent job of "putting it back." It is in the main of Toltec "feathered serpent" influence as opposed to the classic architecture of Uxmal. It is gleamy and shiny. We saw all the Temples and many Chac Mools: the strange stone man with no expression on his face who lies with his knees and head up, a basin on his belly waiting for the bloody hearts of warriors or maidens to be placed, living, thereon, for the eagles to descend and snatch them and bear them up to heaven. I had enjoyed Uxmal, with no eerie feelings. But Chac Mool – ugh . . .
>
> The view as we entered the Great Plaza was like a scene that paints itself: the sculptured temples, all rosy flushed in the sunlight; the pure elongated lines of the Castillo – that is the Temple of Kukulcan (or Quetzlecoatl, the Mexican) and the Temple of the Jaguars. I climbed up to see the jade Jaguar Throne and suddenly realized I couldn't descend the steep

stone stairs. Frozen with terror, I couldn't. A guide saw my dilemma and called me to come down sideways. I had a mad violent urge to dash myself down onto the waiting Chac Mool. I had to force myself to creep down, sideways, sweating, on all fours step by step, step by step.

The Great Ball Court in back of the Jaguar Throne is in fine restoration – the stone "wicket" is hung high up on a stone wall. It is placed horizontally and the players had to butt the ball with their hips through the stone ring. Kingdoms and fortunes of the Maya were lost at Ball games – the Mayas being great gamblers. Near the Ball Court [was] the Tzompantli (cemetery), carved in stone [with] skull faces.

The sun was hot. <u>Many</u> Mexican tourists. Few of <u>us</u>. We walked down the rocky road leading from the Castillo – the summation of the Maya Calendar (the main and tallest temple: 364 stone steps leading up each of the four sides of the perfect pyramid to the temple, making 365, up which the sacrificial victims danced in an orgy of aphrodisiac joy) – to the Sacred Wall of Sacrifice or Cenote, 70 yards in diameter and 60 feet deep with steep unclimbable man-dug-out limestone walls; the water as deep again and shiny pure jade green. Living maidens and beautiful young priests were thrown in the pool as sacrifices to the rain gods, the Chacs. Here I had another feeling – a weird sense of departed spirits – an infinite emptiness, a loneliness, a silence . . .

• • • • •

A few days later, Elizabeth and her friends returned to Merida and checked back into the Pan Americana Hotel. They had signed up for a "How We Live" house tour, a charitable fundraiser sponsored by the Ladies of Merida. Elizabeth delighted at this insider's look into the private world of Mexican aristocracy.

Tuesday, January 22 – At three [pm] we sat down to wait on the padded Victorian sofa in the *Salada Espera* (Hall of Hope – what a nice name for a "waiting" room!) of the hotel. At 3:45 two smartly dressed, petite young ladies arrived. They looked around and began whispering and giggling. I heard the word "Cuckoo" (cuckoo indeed!) – I rose and fixing them with my lorgnette, said crossly, "I am Mrs. Coker. Have you come to take us on your How-We-Live Tour?" The gigglers instantly became aristocratic Yucatecans.

One, in her late twenties with lots of yellow hair piled high on her head, introduced herself as Senora Dona Lia Ponce de Palomeque; the other, about nineteen, a thick platinum spill of hair down to her waist [with] wide, sleepy cornflower blue eyes (if I hadn't realized at a glance that she, luscious now, would be VERY fat later on I might have been jealous, she being about my size and color and all) was Senorita Josefina Peon de Palomeque. The girls explained they were first cousins and this afternoon were going to take us to visit the town houses of their families. (It was only later I learned that Peon and Palmeque equal Middleton in Charleston; Bourbon in France; Windsor in England, and oh well – Coker in Hartsville.)

We drove in Senora Ponce's car to the Plaza Mayor (Main Square in a city of squares). The clay-colored stone cathedral, with its two tall unmatching towers, a gigantic fortress-like structure, was built in the early 16th century. Inside, too, it is very austere. The magnificent *reredos* [an ornamental screen behind an altar] were destroyed in 1915 by revolutionaries. The north and west side of the Plaza are flanked by colonnaded buildings . . . on the south side is Montejo's house, the oldest [extant] dwelling house in America, built by the first conquistador who ruled here. It is painted a soft yellow and on each side of the massive double doorway [are] huge stone figures of armed conquistadores standing on the heads of Indians, representing the conquest of Yucatan. This afternoon the Plaza was filled with Indians and Mexicans and little shoeshine boys and ground doves and trees with a dense and very dark foliage that Senora Lia said were laurel trees.

Senora Lia said her aunt lived in Montejo's house. It took a lot of knocking to rouse a servant. "It's still siesta time," Lia said accusingly to us. A tall lovely, old-fashioned lady who spoke perfect English (as did the girls, both of whom had been to private schools in New York) welcomed us into a wonderful courtyard with tall palms and all sorts of flowering vines and fruiting trees and lilies and roses. An enormous boxer bitch lay snoring in her custom-made sisal hammock; a parrot chattered and a red and blue macaw screamed as we walked (bug-eyed, believe me) along the marble floored arcade, admiring the fine portraits hanging on the stone walls. ("Doesn't it ever rain on them?" I asked. "Oh no – it never blows rain into this sheltered place.")

Chairs of mahogany, cane backed and seated, and sisal hammocks were in groups here and there. The crimson, formal drawing room had a high beamed ceiling and white marble rococo cupids held up heavy red draperies as they sported over the 20-foot-high doorways. "Papa brought the bambinos from Italy when he made the doorways higher," Dona Peon said. "He was very tall." The dining room opening from the arcade was long and crammed with elaborate silver and china and portraits. There was a dim likeness of the merry, ruthless Montejo, who built this house in 1530. "Alas," said Dona Peon, "the name of Montejo disappeared. He had only girls. One married a <u>Peon</u>. Peons have lived in this house ever since" . . .

• • • • •

The group then toured Josefina's house, and finally Lia's, which Elizabeth described as "a typical young modern Yucatan dwelling . . . as neat and jumbled as any young American's house, full of chattering shrieking children and parakeets and nurses." By then everyone was tired, so Elizabeth thanked her hosts and suggested they might return to the hotel. But Josefina announced one final stop on the itinerary: "You are expected for tea at Lia's mother's house," she said. "One of the honest to goodness old-time *grandee* palaces." Elizabeth recounted the memorable visit:

> I wish I could describe Senora Dona Palomeque and her house. To me, she was the essence of old aristocratic Spain. Tight black hair pulled high, flashing black eyes, small, regal; perfect English (she'd been educated in England and Switzerland). She walked very upright, leaning back. Her fingers shone with diamonds. She graciously invited us into her immense (ceilings over 30 feet high, beamed and plastered) drawing room – long stained glass telling the story of Don Quixote windows; much handsomely carved furniture with pink damask seats, imported from Holland; Venetian chandeliers; Blackamoors holding up Venetian glass *torchere* lights; Spanish and Dutch and English religious paintings; cabinets from France, tall vases of Dresden; porcelain from China.
>
> The dining room looked onto a second courtyard. I have never seen such silver except in museums and castles – massive and beautiful. Upstairs the bedrooms in the heavy style of Spain – Huge beds on daises (is there such a word?), masses of crystal and religious cabinets and chairs and Spanish wool rugs. All the doors heavily carved with the doves that are the insignia of the Arms of the Palomeques.
>
> Downstairs again and Dona P said, "Lia, I AM going to show them Papa's study." Lia said, "Oh No." But in Mama took us and there were great black bull heads along the walls and all sorts of bull fighting pictures and picks and swords and capes. It seems that Don P. has two plantations left of his once vast (the vastest in Mexico) family holdings – on one he raises the bulls that fight all over Mexico; on the other, sisal. The old haciendas from these plantations were burned by Juarez [the

> revolutionary]. Oh – Dona P had been to the Bull Fight on Sunday. She said it was a magnificent one . . .

At long last, it was time to say goodbye. Elizabeth expressed their deep gratitude to Senora Dona. The Senora's daughter Lia gathered the Americans in her car for the drive back to the hotel, just as the sun was setting. Elizabeth described the moment in her diary:

> I said – "Look – an El Greco sunset!" The late clouds were black and jagged – the peaked, arched church towers stark white in the late light; and a half moon rode in, mid-sky high and uncaring, above the low black and white horizon.

• • • • •

During their final few days in Yucatan, the group's elegant outfitter, Senor George Garcia Lopez (president of Yucatan Safari, Inc.) invited them to spend a day at his private ranch on the Gulf of Mexico. The plan was to arrive late morning on Thursday, January 24, walk the beach to look for shells and birds, eat lunch, then hunt ducks in the afternoon.

> We drove about an hour through sisal fields and Indian villages, the highway to the sea, to the Indian town of Sisal (where the conquistadores first landed). Here Mario [young Mexican employed by Senor Garcia] stopped and picked up Felipe, an Indian guide, who lay down on a back seat of the jeep and promptly went to sleep and bounced up and down like a rubber log for the hour and a half we drove along the shore on a road (path I'd call it) that was one deep hole and curve after another. Like a jagged roller coaster ride.
>
> But the sea to our right was like a polished sapphire one minute, a faceted emerald the next, in the sparkling sun. A brilliance of birds flew back and forth across the road from the thickets: yellow flycatchers, cardinals, mockers, quail, doves, brown and rosy-painted buntings, vermillion flycatchers, hummingbirds.

Coveys of *chachalacas* kept up a shrill chorus from the growths of trees; man of war birds [frigate birds] flew the sea. Never a house, or a village; but only the sand and the bushes and the palms where they have always been.

Bump – Bounce – Careen. Finally we reached the camp – a clump of wooden cabins, palm thatched, in a planting of banana trees and coconut palms right beside the bright blue sea. [We] immediately started walking up the beach to get the lumps and bumps and kinks out of our poor spines and tails. The shells were wonderful – great pink conchs, striped conchs, little white and orange conchs, angel wings, and all sorts of others I didn't know . . . [at noon] we ate turkey sandwiches and ham and egg sandwiches and bananas and coconut cake soaked in pineapple juice and drank iced orange juice (laced a bit with rum, I must admit) from a thermos . . .

[The group], plus guns and shells and seat cushions and decoys pushed off from a mangrove swamp out onto one of the lagoons that lie back from the sea. Loveliest of all – narry a buzzard – narry a Mr. Chac Mool. Just Felipe and pretty Mario and the roundly rugged Indian . . . This was the finest, and not only the finest, but the loveliest afternooning in the world. Still, though a small wind every now and then, and how bright and clear the water and the surrounding trees! Light came through the leaves like fretted lace; and the clouds were opalescent; the thick mangroves on the water's edge silvery-green . . .

Felipe poled the boat a few miles westward on the lagoon to a place where we halted and took the papier mache decoys (English mallards, if you please) out of sacks and unwound the weights and threw them into a clump on the surface; then we poled over to a mangrove thicket nearby and Felipe got out and waded around and cut branches with his machete and stuck them around the boat, making a fine blind . . . We sat for hours. *Chachalacas* chorused incessantly. Occasionally a *perdiz* [tinamou or partridge] sang . . . We were easy and happy together. Now and then Mario whistled and Felipe called . . .

Around four [pm] a few teal spotted the decoys and came down. Immediately sensing US, up they went – one pretty, one rather slow – the guns spoke – down she came in the middle of the decoys. She struggled to rise and struggled to rise – she lifted her wing – her little tail quivered as if she were trying to set her course – she was still. And the dead decoys, like so many witless-eyed Chac Mools turned with a sudden breeze and put their backs to the little one and in a tight troupe sailed as far away as their strings allowed them, like so many dead soldiers on the march from the living – dying. Then they turned and drifted back and the dead came together, the floating teal one of THEM now. Somewhere a white winged dove called . . . The song was sweet.

Soon came the wings. Clouds and rushes of wings – formations of wings as the ducks poured in and over and there was an endless of shooting and the excitement was high and I could feel ducks on the end of my make-believe gun and my fingers and cheeks itched to be doing it too. Teals, blackhead and widgeons came over, went down, flew past. The sun sank in so many colors it didn't seem true. The half moon was bright in the sky – the evening star was there – so were a million mosquitos. We poled about and began picking up first the decoys then dozens of ducks, and started in.

Then with just the afterglow lighting the sky there came suddenly such a rushing of ducks so low-flying you could feel the air from their wings brush your face. These were the just-over-your-head shots, the on-the-tip-of-your-gun shots. The ones that were black against the afterglow were killed and the others flying into it almost hit us in the face. It was deep dark when we came in. A big wind was blowing over the sea . . .

> A glass of rum relaxed us. Mario came in and had a drink with us. He looked exhausted. He acted strange after his rum and drove the jeep like a madman over the roller coaster sea road. Felipe, fast asleep, rolled about in the back. Every now and then Mario would stop to see if he'd fallen off. Mario was through with us. His job was done. He didn't want to talk and turned the car radio on high with raucous Mexican music. He looked worn out.
>
> One of the Indian villages we passed through was having a fiesta – the girls in their white *huipils,* embroidered in bright flowers, flowers in their hair under their low-crowned Sunday hats – the men all in white – were packed in the village square around a shabby Ferris wheel, lighted booths, a calliope. Some musicians were playing in the market hall and many couples were dancing the *Jarana*. I wanted to stop and mingle, but my suggestion was stonily ignored by everybody. It was ten o'clock when we reached our Pan Americana home. We went in the bar and had some soup and an omelet. Little Elsie had our rooms all turned down. It is very late as I write this. I think I could live happily here forever. Rupert Brook said it better: "Sink slowly to rest – day that I have loved."

• • • • •

Ten months later, in the fall of 1964, Elizabeth returned to Mexico for another hunting safari along the Gulf Coast. Her close attention to natural phenomena and her prowess at shooting were skills she developed growing up in the South Carolina Lowcountry. Like her father, Elizabeth derived peace and vitality from the wild.

> Wednesday, November 18 – Once again [we] are at the ranch of Senior Garcia Lopez on the Gulf of Mexico, south of Sisal (where poor Maximilian and Carlota landed) in Yucatan, Mexico. On the way from Merida, birds in streams of color darted back and forth across the sea road – cardinals, scrub

jays, flycatchers, red and yellow, a *chachalaca* (big and brown as a turkey on a bare tree), great blue herons and many white flocks of willets and pelicans, and a quick little fox after a covey of *cordoniz* (quail) that our jeep flushed.

Our thatched cabin is breezy and cool and comfortable. Serge (a bright Mexican) has fetched soup and steak and fish and fried potatoes for our lunch. Senior Garcia has brought our guns – mine a 410 over and under, similar to one I used to own long ago . . .

Across a stretch of coconut palms the square, white-aproned cook (he does this in between being a bullfighter in Merida and the various nearby villages) is squeezing oranges. [We] are resting a while [before] going duck shooting at 3pm with the Indian and Serge . . . Later, a lovely four hours on the lagoon ending with a full silver moonrise. We saw many egrets, but not a single duck close enough to shoot . . .

Thursday, November 19 – Serge brought coffee at 3:45 [am] pronto. The moonlight was very bright. Dressed by four in my safari garments and to wolf down a breakfast of orange juice, fried eggs, bacon, toast and coffee (very fine) and we were off in the truck with Serge, the Indian, Chalin, boat, guns and shells.

This time we bumped about an hour to a mangrove swamp where the boat was to be put in. A dugout *piroque* [canoe] of a mahogany tree was there. It was dark and mystic pushing through the rooty water to the lagoon, hearing thousands of flamingos waking up along the water side.

The moon, still a solid silver sphere now hung in the West – a brilliant rising Venus challenged from the East. First light began. Duck wings in myriads of whirs and swooshes as we poled toward their sitting places.

> As we reached our mangrove blind the sun's pink fingers reached up to catch Venus. (The first time I ever really saw a "rosy fingered dawn!" Wouldn't have believed it!) The flamingos on the far side glistened. Blue and white herons flew and flew. Little green warblers flitted, etc. The kiskadees' yellow breasts gleamed like satin.
>
> Serge threw out the decoys. Flocks of ducks covered the lake, rose and flew away, [then] settled back down; but adamantly refused to decoy or come near enough for a good shot. At 8 (three hours of standing and stooping) I was allowed to choose and sink a couple of floating shells from some yesterday's gunner and pick a mangrove leaf off a proper tree. But only ten ducks in our bag. And so many flying and sitting as I've never seen or imagined.
>
> Chalin valiantly poled us, for a treat, toward the flamingo flock. There must have been five thousand. Crowds of ducks skimmed and rose and finally a cloud of scarlet-pink flamingos in a wave of shining "beauty bare" in the early sunlight covered us. We picked up lots of their pretty pink feathers floating on the water to fetch home to prove it had been true.

• • • • •

During the summer of 1964, in between travels to Mexico, Elizabeth took her only surviving brother – the physician James Boatwright (P.J.), who was dying of cancer at the time – to Turkey. Their mission? To dissuade Elizabeth's niece Betsy – James' 23-year-old daughter, who was teaching at the Robert College school in Istanbul – from hastily entering into marriage with a young Turk.

Upon arriving at the airport in Istanbul on Saturday, June 27, "up rushed Betsy," Elizabeth wrote in her diary.

> . . . black eyes asparkle, gold hair aswing; and who was this gorgeous young gentleman with her? Not HE – the terrible

> Turk? Surely this young edition of Charles Boyer [the French-American film star] in a crisp grey silk suit and shiny black shoes, bowing over my hand, speaking perfect English – surely THIS was not our villainous Attila? What a surprise!

"Daddy, Aunt Elizabeth," exclaimed Betsy, "Oh, I'm so thrilled to see you. Attila, didn't I tell you how beautiful they were? Didn't I, Attila?"

Elizabeth recounted their first hours together:

> Attila and my brother careened off in his powerful Morgan sports car. Betsy drove with me in the antique limousine I had prearranged to meet us in case Attila turned out to be – ! Everything was wonderful to Betsy; but she warned me not to mention the words Cypress or Greece: "The Turks hate all Greeks <u>and</u> Greece. Don't even refer to your going there from here."

"What am I doing here?" Elizabeth wondered.

> Why, I came to rescue our pretty child from a fate worse than death and here I find Attila-bey!! Brother J and I, relieved of our burden, rested well and sunset came and I went down and sat on the hotel terrace. Handsome, richly dressed people walked up and down and sat and drank the smoky Turkish liquor they call *raki* or Turkish coffee – served by a dark-eyed girl in the gauzy Turkish trousers, veil and fez of Aladdin's time.

"At seven, the beautiful young returned," continued Elizabeth.

> My brother came down looking handsome and rested. I had a martini (<u>here</u> of all places!), Brother J a glass of *raki*, Betsy and Attila a sip of coffee. Attila is worldly and smooth. <u>She</u> is all sparkle and excitement . . . Lights twinkled around the Bosphorous [Strait], kind dark descended – the long day that was to have been loud with dramatic, ugly edicts dwindled into sleepily pleasant goodnights. Ah – a great blue jar of lilies

> (sent by Attila) spills sweetness in my room. I have four huge wonderful down pillows on my bed. I sink deliciously away from the world – hopefully for a thousand nights and a night!

The next morning the phone rang in Elizabeth's hotel room. It was a Mrs. Carp from the American Legation. At Elizabeth's request, she had "looked up" Attila Goksel – investigating his family, character, etc. Mrs. Carp relayed her report: "The University of Istanbul where he teaches [Ph.D. in engineering] considers him to have a brilliant future. He is greatly esteemed . . . He is of the ancient Ottoman aristocracy; his grandfather lived in the Sultan's palace – an aristocrat of much honor . . . And so on and so on."

As Elizabeth noted later, "What had loomed as a tragedy became a delight . . . We'd come this far in a fury and here is a love story straight out of the Arabian Nights!"

Over the next few days, Attila and Betsy and Attila's mother showed Elizabeth and James the sights of Istanbul: the great mosque of Suleyman the Magnificent, the ancient Bazaar of Constantinople, the Topkapi Palace, and the Dolmabahce Palace – built by Sultan Abdulmecid I and containing 285 rooms and 46 halls. Another day they took "a peasant type trip in a ferry boat up the Bosphorous Strait [to have] lunch *al fresco* in a fisherman's cove."

One evening, Betsy and Attila hosted everyone for supper at Attila's apartment, high on a hill by the shores of the Bosphorous, near the ruins of the Castle of Rumeli Hissar [a medieval fortress guarding the strait]. "Attila-bey came for us at six and we drove out to Rumeli Hissar, where he lives in a little penthouse apartment that looks over the Bosphorous, the Golden Horn and all [of] Istanbul," wrote Elizabeth in her journal. "Betsy waited on us at the top of the winding stair (four steep flights we trudged) and we sat on the terrace drinking a smooth white wine and eating pistachio nuts and cherries, apricots and green plums." She went on to observe:

> Ships went up and down. Attila had lovely music (taped) that fitted in with the wine . . .
>
> Betsy brought out the supper – a pilaf of rice, cinnamon, raisins, pine nuts, lamb; a platter of broiled steak; a salad of cucumbers, lettuce, black olives; eggplant and whole hot pep-

pers broiled in olive oil; a dish of raw hot peppers; another bottle of wine. Dusk dropped down and rosy lights, like pink amethysts, flashed up and down the high round hills and up and down the Bosphorous. Across is Asia – this side Europe.

For dessert, we had *baklava* (a honey pastry) and then Turkish coffee in thin little glasses. Talk remained good – the mood mellow – except when a Viennese waltz came on the tape and Attila dared me (or did I dare him?) to take a whirl around the terrace. (He's a marvelous dancer.)

I guess it was the whirling dance – anyway, afterwards I floated on my high heels down the steps and on down a steep rocky incline – dark and mysterious, winding between tall dark houses to the street where Attila hailed a taxi and he and Betsy escorted us back to the Hilton.

I to save Betsy? Hoo – 'tis Betsy who should come to Hartsville and save me!

Chapter 14

A FEELING HEART

"These things are permanent to me. I have a feeling heart. I treasure them!"

– Elizabeth Boatwright Coker

All through life, Elizabeth embraced her duties as wife and mother, daughter and niece, sister and aunt, grandmother and great aunt, with energy, humor and compassion. In one of the many interviews she gave as a bestselling author in the 1950s, she describes balancing her myriad familial responsibilities with her demanding professional career:

> It was not until 1947, after having married and raised a daughter to the ripe old age of fifteen and a son to the unripe age of six, that I really began the borning [birth of her first novel, *Daughter of Strangers*]. Penelope, my daughter, was away at boarding school. Jamesy, my little boy, spent his mornings in public school. I had a cook. My husband betook himself to his mill by 9am. It looked to be the perfect setup.
>
> And it was – except that there never is any proper time to sit down at the typewriter and write. I have heard women writers say smugly – "Oh I sit down to write every day from nine until twelve and then again from two until four-thirty; come out and have a cocktail and leisurely dinner, after which some friends drop in and we talk about literature until bedtime."
>
> I look on these writers with awe and disbelief. What do they do when the phone rings? When callers come? What if their husbands don't want to talk about literature every night? Of course, a man writer always has a gentle little woman who dotes on him to protect him from the cruel world . . .

> The telephone is the arch enemy of creative aspiration. I daren't not answer it. It might be word that Penelope's horse has fallen over a fence out hunting in some wild and dreadful forest; it might be that one of those nasty big boys at school has bloodied little James' cute button of a nose; it probably is my husband saying he is bringing four of his most important customers home to lunch and please see that the spoons are shiny and the flowers bright.

Several years later, when asked about her children, Elizabeth gave the following update – told with a blend of affection and amusement:

> I have two children, a daughter, Penelope, 27 years old. She is tall, dark and handsome, an accomplished horsewoman and, thank the Lord, has a wonderful Irish sense of the ridiculous inherited from my mother. At present, she is working in New York as Cleveland Amory's "girl Friday."
>
> My other child is a red-haired son, James IV, 18 [years old], who has just graduated from Woodberry Forest School in Virginia and who keeps me limber by making me do the Charleston with him, and try unsuccessfully to learn to water ski so people won't think he has an antique and queer writer for a mother.

• • • • •

Like his father, James IV went on to the University of North Carolina and Harvard Business School, and ultimately into the family business. His memories of Elizabeth and Jim are vivid and lasting:

> As a little boy, I was read to constantly by Ma and Pa – stories like *Winnie-the-Pooh*, stories of the ancient gods and goddesses, history stories, stories from the Bible, poetry. They taught me the importance of loving and caring for and protecting others – that honesty and caring, and giving help and comfort to others, was what the world needed.

In addition to this depth and strength, and the importance of these lessons of love and support and goodness, I became aware, particularly in Ma, of a fierceness and control; coupled with a wonderful enjoyment and laughter. There was a sense of humor and enjoyment within her which she expressed beautifully.

Throughout my entire experience with Ma, I could see that she loved life; and no matter what might be going on, she continued to enjoy and take pleasure in living, traveling, working, writing, socializing and pursuing her many interests.

Let me start with Ma's absolute happiness and strength in driving cars. We grew up with two automobiles in our home. One was Pa's Cadillac, and the other was Ma's Buick. In 1954, when the first Corvette came out, Pa bought one for Ma. She obviously loved to drive it, and whenever she would take me to school or to music lessons or wherever, she would drive it fiercely and with great glee.

Every four years, Ma would trade the Corvette in and get a new one. It was always yellow, always four-speed shift, always high power – as in eight cylinders. She drove like holy hell.

Ma liked to shoot and had a 34 revolver. Often, she would get James Lunn – our yard and chauffeur and fixit man – to put cans and bottles on top of the trash pile in the backyard. With all the staff watching, she would, at 30 yards back, shoot and knock off each object that James put on the pile. As a young boy growing up and observing this, I knew she was fierce.

Her fierceness manifest itself in her enjoyment of doing things she liked and at which she was good. At the same time, this fierceness enabled her to deal with hard and distressing events – challenges she experienced and that her loved ones experienced – such as caring for Pa when he came down with cancer. With her help, he recovered sufficiently – albeit temporarily

> – to be able to live happily for several years. When he died in 1961, I was 20 years old and Penelope was 29. Ma's strength helped us get through this heartbreaking time.
>
> Ma was strict, enforcing rules with precision and strength, out of a motivation to protect and train and care for, in particular, the men in her life. I learned much of this through her writings, as many of her characters were sweet and smart men, who needed to be protected and loved.
>
> I began to observe and experience these characteristics in Ma many years before I truly understood them. Over my lifetime, I have learned from and cherished more and more the profound beauty and essence of these central elements of her spirit, and the way in which she conveyed them to me.

A graduate of Sarah Lawrence College, Penelope would rise from "girl Friday" to senior editor and biographer of Cleveland Amory's *Celebrity Register*. Later in the 1960s and 70s, she worked as a reporter and producer for local television stations, first in Philadelphia and then in New York – cohosting "The New Yorkers" daytime show and anchoring the Channel Five Sunday news. She was one of the first women to host a daytime TV talk show in the United States. In 1964, she married film producer William Wilson. Their daughter Eliza was born in 1968.

Penelope also wrote children's books and co-authored with Ann LaFarge (former editor at E.P. Dutton) the novel *Riding High* under the pseudonym of Emily Brooks. Later she became editor of *Dutchess Magazine* and served on the boards of numerous educational institutions and arts organizations. She remains a member of the Screen Actors Guild.

Penelope conveys the ups and downs, the joys and contradictions, of life with Elizabeth Boatwright Coker:

> EBC had two children, nine years apart; and I am the only person here who can claim the title of EBC's daughter. Of course, James is here, but he is a boy and came much later.

> But I was the one who got practiced on. I was the one who, when EBC went to a summer graduate writing gathering at Middlebury College, was put into a Yankee camp in Vermont for two months at the age of six. I was the one whose mother came to Parents' Day in shorts. But back to the contradictions: Some days before a teenage party, EBC would say, "You look marvelous!" Other days it would be, "You're not wearing THAT?"
>
> She was 41 when Dutton published her book *Daughters of Strangers* to fine reviews. She had written a bestseller, the first of many. She went from strength to strength, always reveling in this beloved state: Writing, Traveling, Speaking, Laughing all the way.
>
> Her success had made her stronger, gentler, more beautiful; her kindness reached the heights, and she cared lovingly and tirelessly for her courageous beloved Jim when he was attacked by a vicious illness – during which, in his way and with her help, he was able to work and travel. She was always at his side; he was not cured but he conquered.
>
> Still, EBC never stopped writing. She produced [nine] novels, countless articles; she taught, and made wonderful speeches. In fact, she became more and more successful.
>
> But all was not work and serious contemplation. She had a famously outrageous sense of humor. She could tell a slightly off-color mountain story in perfect dialect that would make you hoot, and the next day, enjoy a lunch with the bishop, extolling the often overlooked virtues of John the Baptist . . .

• • • • •

When Elizabeth's brother William died in 1952, she assumed responsibility for his three children's education. She did the same for her brother

James' daughters when he fell ill with cancer. Elizabeth believed fervently in the importance of a good education, as illustrated in this excerpt from her 1987 commencement address to the graduates of Coker College, the school founded by Jim's grandfather:

> [Napoleon] Bonaparte once asked Madame de Stael in what manner he could best promote the happiness of the French people.
>
> She replied: "Instruct the mothers and fathers of the French people. For mothers and fathers are the most affectionate and most effective teachers of the human race."
>
> If there is one permanent idea that you carry away with you today, let it be this: to pour on the heads of your children the instruction that has been your privilege at Coker College. You owe them that Baptism.

As her nieces and nephews grew into adulthood, they stayed in close touch with their famous aunt. Elizabeth explained the family situation in her characteristic forthright manner, recognizing her good fortune of having an income.

> I began writing for money when I become a professional writer, that is to say when I absolutely settled on a career as a writer and signed a contract with my publisher. This was very fortunate for I have had to accept the financial responsibility of the children of my two brothers. The three children of my older brother (who died in 1952) have been supported entirely by me with the gain from writing. I sent them all to college. The elders each for four years, the youngest for two. I also was forced, by circumstance, to educate the two daughters of my younger brother. I sent them four years to Agnes Scott with the gain from my literary efforts. This may answer your question as to why I wrote for profit, though my husband was able to support me. Another reason I write for profit is

> because without profit there is no incentive; and now with no husband, I need the money to help pay my bills and assist my brother, who is very ill.

Once the younger generation had families of their own, Elizabeth followed closely the lives of her great nieces and nephews, as well as that of her granddaughter, Eliza. She exuded pride in their accomplishments as young high school and college students, illustrated in this passage from a 1985 letter:

> First and most precious, of course, Penelope's daughter, Eliza. She attended the summer school of dance at Duke University emerging radiant with accomplishment and loving as ever. [Eliza would go on to graduate from Middlebury College, become a professional dancer and choreographer, and a professor of dance at the College of Charleston.] Next, there was my brother William's granddaughter, Carrie, a junior at Clemson University majoring in nuclear physics, who worked here in Hartsville at the nuclear power plant out on Lake Robinson – the top summer trainee job of any college student in South Carolina. In addition to being a brain, she is also lovely to look at and charming to be with . . . Last but by no means least, my brother James' half-Turkish granddaughter – Dilara Goksel of Istanbul [daughter of Betsy Boatwright and Attila Goksel, whom Elizabeth and James visited in the summer of 1964]. Two months past 15, she was taken by the headmaster of one of the most prestigious prep schools in the U.S. (he had taught her in Turkey at Robert College Lower School) to be interviewed at Williams, Wellesley, Princeton and Davidson. She was offered scholarships by each one for the next year, provided she keeps up her brilliant progress!

• • • • •

Family meant ancestors and Southern heritage too. Stories and remembrances of the ancestors were recited over and over, bringing them to life for Elizabeth, her brothers and their cousins. In a 1979 commencement address at her alma mater, Converse College, Elizabeth referenced the influence of family history and storytelling:

> I have continued to write with tumultuous enthusiasm about "things I am familiar with" and made every effort to portray my characters vividly and honestly, sometimes pitilessly without becoming, and I quote Thomas Wolfe, shaken by the fury which Asheville heaped on him in 1929 when *Look Homeward Angel* was published: *A carrion crow preying on the blood and bones of my relatives and friends, an unnatural ghoul to whom nothing is sacred, not even the tombs of the honored dead . . . a rattlesnake, a jackass, an alley cat and a baboon.* [often referred to as the "betrayal that is writing"]
>
> . . . The really scandalous problems or happenings, those too delicate to discuss on the front porch in front of the children were talked [about] out on the back porch with a few close relatives. It was true group therapy. You pay for such psychic luxury nowadays!
>
> My grandfather Boatwright was one of the heroes of Gettysburg; my great grandmother coped with a great many slaves, too many babies and a vast cotton plantation at one and the same time. My four times great grandfather, Michael Watson, was a doughty Indian fighter. There is a tall marble column marking the spot where he fell, pierced by dozens of arrows, near Orangeburg, S.C. His son scampered around in the South Carolina swamps during the Revolution with General Francis Marion. George Washington put it in writing that the freshest, prettiest faces to greet him on his Southern tour were the Misses Watsons of Old Edgefield!
>
> I grew up on stories about these people and their descendants – the laughter and tears and failures and triumphs that carried them through the generations. I have one of the thin cameo earrings my great-great-grandfather gave his bride on their

> wedding day. My New York granddaughter was baptized in the exquisite christening gown made for my father in Charleston, S.C. In 1869, the cane with which one of my great uncles thrashed a man who kicked one of his hunting dogs is still in the umbrella stand at Shady Branch. Grandmother's piano music includes the first printing of Strauss' "Blue Danube," as well as the first printings of "The Secession March" and "Dixie's Land."
>
> These things are permanent to me. I have a feeling heart. I treasure them!

In her address, she expounded further on the legacy of history and storytelling in Southern literature:

> At the National Booksellers Association last June I was on the *New York Times* panel discussion with five other Southern writers and newspapermen. We agreed that it is impossible to envision a Southern literature without the strong influence of what has gone before.
>
> Young Southern writers will always be drawn back to a real past. We have a shared past, a profound sense of the past. I am talking about the importance of history when I say this. And face it, we Southerners <u>are</u> a race of storytellers, myth worshippers and local bards. Regard the current vogue of country music. Most of the songs are pure short stories in rhythm! Sam Stoney used to ask: "How do South Carolinians differ from Chinamen? Answer: The Chinese worship their ancestors and eat rice. South Carolinians eat their ancestors and worship rice."
>
> Well I've fattened off mine. They flit in and out of all my books, even the modern one, *The Bees*, in which I incorporate the story of my grandfather Boatwright. He was with Lee at Appomattox Courthouse, where Lee, in an immaculate new

> gray uniform, was meeting with Grant, [who was] in an old soiled blue uniform. When word sifted out that Lee had actually surrendered, my grandfather drew his cavalry sword from its scabbard and stuck it into a nearby tree stump, swearing an oath never to draw it out in war again. Then without looking back, he mounted his black horse and galloped away for home.
>
> So how can I not see history as high romance? A sword in a stump is not too far removed from an Arthurian sword in a stone.

• • • • •

Elizabeth was a natural-born storyteller, but she understood that translating stories into literature was hard work. Good writing was a well-honed craft and an art – requiring relentless study and practice, constant revising and fine-tuning. On the publication of *Daughter of Strangers*, she commented to an interviewer on her writing process:

> I determined from the start not to let any of my pages go out into the world until they were as well written as I knew how to write them. I tried not to write carelessly, nor to express my ideas crudely. I wanted terribly to be a good craftsman for I have always faced up to the fact that writing is not hackwork which can be picked up at random, but an art which must be mastered.
>
> Another condition I accepted was that those authors who write only when they are "inspired" must take many years to complete their books.
>
> I find it essential to write whether I have an inspiration or whether I don't. Not even Joan of Arc heard voices <u>every</u> day. I write whenever it is physically possible. Yet I rarely go with light steps to my red simulated leather and aluminum kitchen chair and sit at the scarred card table which bears

my typewriter. Rather I dilly and dally wondering what in the world am I going to say today? Will Charlotte and Inigo become lovers? Shall I let the sun shine gently, or must the harsh March wind ruin all the ladies' *frizets*?

The first few sentences each day are usually inadequate and inane, but before long the enchantment takes hold awakening me into a new and clean vision of what my story might become. This enchantment is like some strange spell, but it is so strong and so consumingly interesting that my 40th birthday passed without a qualm, even though at the time I was in the process of rewriting *Daughter of Strangers* for the third time.

As a matter of fact, I write everything three times. First I sit at the typewriter and get my ideas down as quickly as possible and at long length. Getting them down is the most important step of all, imprisoning them in print.

Secondly, I pull what I have written closer together; telescope, as it were, the content into the fewest possible words. Sometimes a chapter of 25 pages in the first draft turns up with only ten in the second.

And third, I polish. Every sentence, every phrase, is weighed to see if it could be said more effectively or more beautifully. This last process is where the fun comes in. The first two writings are endurance tests, but the final job of gilding the lily makes you <u>feel</u> like a writer.

The research is great fun [too]. Most of mine was done in the Caroliniana room at the University of South Carolina Library, but a great deal was done in my own collection acquired from my good friend Mr. Gittman [of Gittman's Book Shop] in Columbia – in the same manner that some women hunt for and discover sandwich glass or Victorian sofas or rare camellias.

• • • • •

As an author, Elizabeth represented a direct link to a flowering of literature and art in South Carolina which took place in the 1920s, 30s and 40s – called the Charleston Renaissance – which anticipated and helped precipitate similar movements across the South. Much younger than most of the Renaissance writers and artists, Elizabeth knew them later in life. According to Harlan Greene, co-editor of *Renaissance in Charleston: Art and Life in the Carolina Low Country*, she carried their torch "on into time . . . into a different era and a different city."

"Yet her *Daughter of Strangers* has a title that is a throwback to the Renaissance," Greene asserts. "It's inheritance here, too; the shock of prejudice and injustice . . . through her heroine, [the author] was doing just what the renaissance artists were – trying to deal with a world their parents had come from, and one they could not live in comfortably."

In a 1960 speech entitled "Remembrance of South Carolina Writers Past," Elizabeth paid tribute to this cultural rebirth, and especially to those writers who had mentored and encouraged her:

> My first real memory of a South Carolina writer is of DuBose Heyward in 1918 or 1919. He was in Darlington to sell insurance. Daddy brought him home to midday dinner. He was a thin knife of a person weakened by polio, with deep dark eyes and a birdlike set of his head. When he left, Mama fussed, "He never said a word the whole meal." Daddy said, "He's in the wrong business."
>
> Another gentleman felt the same way: Mr. John Bennett, whose lovely book *Skylark* [*Master Skylark*] had been a great hit in the 1890s. [He] had married a Charleston lady, moved to her city and quickly become a dyed-in-the-wool Charlestonian. He took an intense interest in DuBose Heyward and Hervey Allen, both of whom had had a few stories and poems accepted by small publications.
>
> A professor at Porter Military Academy [in Charleston], Hervey

> Allen hailed from Pittsburgh, Pennsylvania. He sucked a pipe and looked like a giant Norseman of olden days. Mr. Bennett masterminded the Poetry Society of South Carolina primarily to push his two protégées [Heyward and Allen] into careers and as professional writers. They called themselves "The Three Musketeers" . . . From the very beginning the Poetry Society was touched with magic. . . . Following its lead, writers groups with little magazines flared up all over the South.
>
> This little Society launched not only Heyward and Allen into writing careers, but also Josephine Pinckney, Beatrice Ravenel, Katherine Drayton Mayrant Simons and others; and encouraged, in particular, such young poets as Donald Davidson, Leonora Speyer, Robert Penn Warren and William Alexander Percy . . . In 1928, I received Mr. Bennett's Skylark Prize offered by the Poetry Society of South Carolina for the best poem by a college student.
>
> Josephine Pinckney had succeeded DuBose Heywood as president of the Society she loved so well. But it was the elegant old man Mr. Bennett himself, who hugged me after [the awards ceremony] was all over and loudly wished he was twenty-one again so he could marry me and live happily ever after on all the money I was sure to make as a writer.

Even the "very private" and "self-possessed" Josephine Pinckney (author of *Three O'clock Dinner*) – someone Elizabeth wished she had known better – "was gracious and encouraging about my future as a writer." But her most important mentor in the Poetry Society was South Carolina author and fellow Converse graduate Julia Peterkin. Like Elizabeth, Peterkin didn't publish her first book until she was in her forties. And like Elizabeth, she produced bestsellers – including the 1929 Pulitzer Prize-winning novel, *Scarlet Sister Mary.*

• • • • •

Elizabeth remained loyal to her hometown of Darlington and her adopted communities of Hartsville and Blowing Rock, even as she was celebrated around the country and the world. Throughout her career, she was a faithful letter writer to countless old friends and family members, while also maintaining correspondence with luminaries of the literary world, including Norman Mailer and John Jakes. Jakes penned the following words to Elizabeth in the spring of 1982, just as the first volume of his famous trilogy, *North and South,* was topping *The New York Times* bestseller list:

> Your latest letter was grand – and, in the final paragraph, beautifully touching. I, too, feel that I have found a dear friend in you: as I may have said, there is hardly another writer about whom I would say that; most of the time, I would prefer to spend my time with anyone but a writer . . . how grand to find, among the other beautiful benefits of this island [Hilton Head, where Jakes and his wife moved in 1978] a jewel of an exception in you.

Jakes was exploring a potential collaboration with Elizabeth to turn her 1977 novel *Blood Red Roses* into a musical. Jakes loved writing for the musical theater. He also loved his island home of Hilton Head, where *Blood Red Roses* was set.

> I've already discussed the book with my collaborator, composer Gil Martin of New York; Gil has a long and outstanding history of choral composition, acting and musical direction for the theater (and we have written six shows together). He agrees with me that BRR [*Blood Red Roses*] would make a highly engaging musical, in the vein of Shenandoah of a few years ago.

Jakes followed up with Elizabeth a few months later. His analysis of *Blood Red Roses*, especially its heroine, Angel, affirms why Elizabeth's characters resonated with her readers. Jakes' commentary on discovering "the essence . . . the core . . . the backbone" of a narrative is both a beautiful literary treatise and a testament to the universality and power of Elizabeth's storytelling.

First off, I must say your idea for an opening suggests that you may have missed one of your callings – dramatist. It sounds eminently workable, and coincides with much of what I've written in my annotated copy of the book.

The first problem, or challenge, in putting a show together is to discover what the show is really about – what is the simple word or two which sums up its essence? If you can't find that, you wander all over the place and ultimately fail.

The classic example is Fiddler on the Roof. It is really not about being Jewish in Russia in the late 19th century; it is about change, as epitomized in the generation gap – and insiders say the show never jelled until director Jerome Robbins "discovered" this; the opening number, "Tradition," which pulls the whole show together and gives it direction, was not written until well along in rehearsals.

In the same way, I have been searching for the core of our show – and what I think it is, at this stage anyway, is not the Civil War, or Hilton Head Island (though those are fascinating backgrounds, just as the village of Anatevka is fascinating in Fiddler). What I think we have as a "universal" in this show is the struggle (on the part of the heroine) to survive. Survival is what it's all about – and not just survival in war (though that of course is part of our specific story). Not everyone must learn to survive in a war, but everyone must learn to survive – and that is a magnificent universal "backbone" for our musicalized story whose concrete color and detail come from Hilton Head in war.

Angel is a classic heroine for the musical stage – and for this particular story of survival: she is a sheltered girl when the story starts; a tough, sinewy survivor when it ends and Beau comes home. That is a wonderful transition for a character in a musical play – and the greater the adversities she faces, the

> harder we'll root for her.
>
> Anyway, I wanted to answer your good note before I left, tell you that I like what you said – and raise this question of what the "Method" acting school calls the spine of the show: for if you don't have it, and have it clearly, you write aimlessly – which is what I don't want to do.
>
> But as I said to myself when I noted "survival" on one of the frontmatter pages of my copy – "By George, I think he's got it." Hope you think so too.

• • • • •

Elizabeth had become that "finder of a rarer gem" – "a sayer." Writing provided the portal through which she could wholly embrace and illuminate life – getting to the heart of the human condition in all its joy and sorrow and beauty. Her love for and faith in writing, where the self and the soul could find full expression, was her polestar. She articulated her calling in the following journal entry:

> A writer is a blender of horizons into new shapes, a finder of a rarer gem in a new place, a sayer of how we mortals lived and loved and died, how we saw each other, how we sought and lost our God and how we suddenly one day found and knew that though life is a short thing– a changing thing – there is hope, there is much beauty and kindness, much goodness and things of real value here for us if we just will refuse to turn our backs on life; but will savor every different phase of it as it comes up on it.

Chapter 15

FINAL CHAPTER

In December of 1979 Elizabeth underwent a mastectomy. She approached breast cancer with her usual forthrightness and optimism, as illustrated in the following letter written to her good friend Ann LaFarge, editor at E.P. Dutton:

> Dear Ann –
>
> By now you have probably learned of the holocaust that has engulfed me since mid-December. I haven't announced the lurid details of my mastectomy to anyone at Dutton and ask you not to.
>
> I had a Xmas card from Susan, but have not heard a word from Dutton [regarding *The Grasshopper King*] since the great god Corn [Chuck Korn] took over. I haven't pushed, waiting till my strength returned to try and accomplish anything.
>
> Oh – my prognosis for the future is excellent. It's the hideous here and now that's so hard.
>
> I'd love to see you. If you're ever nearby – pay me a visit. I'll have to come to N.Y. to check with my doctors from time to time and of course we'll always have Millbrook to share.
>
> Do send me news of you, dear friend, and also of your talented children.
>
> Love and a happy 1980 to you!
>
> Elizabeth

Two years later she lost a dear friend, writer and editor Jonathan Daniels, who had been a classmate of author Thomas Wolfe at the University of North Carolina. Daniels understood the gifted, glamorous author better than anyone. He adored her, and his poetry showed it, as in this verse he penned when Elizabeth underwent surgery soon after Jim's death.

Across your rugs and up your stair
Must be a fairy kingdom where
All mark of hurt, of stress, of years
By some sweet magic disappears.
Yet you insist that I should note
The thin pink line upon your throat,
And then say lightly, like a dare,
"Old friend, remember, Death was there."

I do recall it was the knife
That in skilled fingers saved your life,
Yet left you strangely with the will
With your skilled hands to hunt and kill
The wild white pigeons that you know
Wheel in the skies of Mexico.
Elegant huntress, I see you stand,
Triumphant in sport in Yucatan,
Accepting the praises of your guide
For the pile of pigeons by your side.
But note, my lady, gun at rest,
Red wounds upon the still white breast
Of the rumpled thing that was a bird
Until your splendid gun was heard.
They seemed to dance upon the air,
Flying, wheeling, unaware
That Death, my dear, is everywhere.
That blotch of blood upon your dress
Is no good reason for distress.
There is not the slightest doubt
That in skilled hands it will wash out.

On Thursday, November 12, 1981, the following letter to the editor appeared in *The Island Packet*, the Hilton Head Island newspaper that Daniels had founded:

> To *The Packet*:
> Oh weep for Jonathan's friends – he is dead. The throne of the king is empty; Calibogue Court closed; the Round Table hushed. Our brightest bird with the strongest song has flown. The ocean tides still come in and go out as is their rhythm. But a handful of island sand has washed away and cannot come again. We are less.
>
> Elizabeth Boatwright Coker

• • • • •

Unbowed, Elizabeth returns to where our story began – the Franklin Delano Roosevelt Presidential Library in Hyde Park, New York. It is the winter of 1983-1984 and once again she is seated at her favorite table in the main reading room. She isn't dwelling on the past. Instead she is working on a new book: a biography of Sara Delano Roosevelt, the late president's mother. She has agreed to write it at the request of FDR's son Franklin D. Roosevelt, Jr. – Penelope and Morti Hall's neighbor in Millbrook.

At a dinner party over Christmas, Franklin, Jr., approached Elizabeth about collaborating on a book project. Well aware of the author's brilliance and popularity, he followed up with a letter on December 27th: "I am delighted that you think well of doing a book on my grandmother's life – perhaps in historical novel form. Perhaps after the holiday festivities we can get together and discuss it seriously."

In the new year, Franklin, Jr., invited Elizabeth to lunch at his home. To her delight, he quickly got down to business. His dazzling Roosevelt smile indicated that the deal was done. Soon afterwards they signed a collaboration agreement.

She wondered how Jim would view this new partnership. Like most Southerners in the first half of the 20th century, the Cokers had traditionally voted Democratic, but switched parties in the 1940 presidential election to support FDR's opponent, Republican Wendell Willkie.

No matter how much their personal, business and political lives were scrutinized, nothing seemed to dim the Roosevelts' ebullient attitude. Elizabeth, cut from the same cloth, connected with Franklin, Jr., immediately.

She understood that the primary purpose of the book was to dispel misperceptions and resurrect Sara Roosevelt's public image. From the beginning, fate had cast Sara and her daughter-in-law Eleanor into an adversarial relationship. When FDR and Eleanor became engaged, Sara had vehemently disapproved and tried to change her son's mind. Undeterred, FDR married Eleanor in 1905, despite his mother's view that she was unworthy of him. (A number of Eleanor's family and friends thought he was unworthy of her.) However, FDR and Eleanor never created a home that was independent of Sara. She inserted herself into every facet of their family affairs except one – the couple's public life. Sara detested the political arena and would have nothing to do with it.

Nonetheless, she showered affection on her grandchildren and created a rich and loving home life for them at Hyde Park, the Roosevelt family seat. She also supported her daughter-in-law after Eleanor discovered in 1918 that FDR and Lucy Mercer were having an affair. As the first lady recalled years later, "The bottom dropped out of my own particular world, and I faced myself, my surroundings, my world, honestly for the first time."

Collaborating with Franklin, Jr., and putting aside an unfinished novel, was an easy decision for Elizabeth. How to elevate perceptions of Sara without damaging Eleanor's reputation was more challenging. An expert in interpreting the nuances of human relationships – set against historical backdrops of war, political intrigue and socioeconomic upheaval – Elizabeth tackled the project with her typical intensity.

Day after day at the FDR Library, archivists delivered one folder after another to the master storyteller as she took notes in her steno pad. "When I write," Elizabeth explained to a friend, "I get just dead serious."

• • • • •

Suddenly, the closing bell rings and jolts Elizabeth out of her trance-like focus. She gathers up notes and pencils, straightens materials for re-shelving, retrieves her pocketbook, and bids goodbye to the librarians. Outside, a ray of light sweeps through the trees and across the library grounds, one last bright streak of yellow-gold before the setting sun disappears behind the western hills.

Elizabeth sits on a bench waiting for Penelope to fetch her home for cocktail hour in front of the fire. The chill and clarity of the atmosphere are refreshing. She smiles thinking about her beautiful, talented, devoted daughter, who sees to her every need and makes sure she is never bored. A steady stream of invitations – to horse shows, cocktail parties, luncheons, dinners, book signings, charity events – is issued and received weekly.

Inevitably though, Elizabeth awaits her return to the library. Not that she doesn't enjoy the whirl of Millbrook, social being that she is. It's that familiar tension between the demands of family and society, and the irresistible pull of writing. She knows her research and writing keep her centered; much as daughter Penelope and granddaughter Eliza keep her grounded. Elizabeth has worked hard her entire career to strike a balance.

• • • • •

In the spring of 1983, prior to the advent of the Roosevelt book proposal, Elizabeth and Penelope traveled to Indonesia on a six-week voyage with the National Trust. It was the last major overseas trip for Elizabeth and one of the most memorable. The journey began with high drama and hilarity, much to the delight of the well-heeled group of travelers.

> April 6 – Singapore. The flight to Singapore on Singapore Airlines took 26 hours, but the plane was comfortable; the caviar and champagne excellent; the totally reclining seats soft; the service silky smooth. The Hotel Dynasty, where we arrived two days after leaving New York, at 3am, is a vast expanse of gilt and crimson set amid towering skyscrapers and frantic noisy machines tearing down everything old and building up new cubes and triangles of steel and glass. Nothing is allowed to remain in Singapore that isn't at least eight stories tall; not even the venerable section called "Chinatown" itself. There is nothing Chinesey about anywhere – not even a Chinese symbol or word in the gargantuan modern airport.

> Tonight, at six, when Penelope and I walked into the "get together" party at the hotel, hosted by the National Trust, everybody crowded around me exclaiming "How do you do it?" "What? What?" cried I. "How can you look so young and be ninety-three years old?" "I'm seventy-three, not ninety-three!" I shouted furiously.
>
> The head of the group apologetically explained how the National Trust had had many sessions trying to decide whether to let me come along or not at my advanced age, but since my daughter was accompanying me, they reluctantly decided to give me a try. What a beginning! At least everyone has noticed me . . .

Aboard the *M.V. Illiria* – exploring Bali, Java, Komodo and other islands of the Indonesian archipelago – the mix of nature, culture and history was right up Elizabeth's alley. She described the adventure in a letter to friends:

> Sixty of us sailed aboard a tiny Greek ship – more of a big yacht. I was far and away the oldest, but managed to reach the tips of the volcanoes and the summit of the Ninth Century Temple of Borobudur in Java first, and with the easiest breathing . . .

Elizabeth celebrated her 74th birthday (April 21st) while on the trip, and was toasted – and roasted – by her fellow passengers at dinner one night. The following poem, entitled "To the Yellow Bird of Larantuka, on her so-called 93rd Birthday," was composed and recited by newfound friend and admirer the Reverend W. Brown Morton III:

> In Manhattan stylish rakes
> Have been known to make mistakes
> But no gaff was ever bigger
> Than the one which we now figure
> Made a birthday sum too great
> And transported a natal date!

A CURIOUS HEART

A fellow of antique extraction
Prey to manual distraction
Dreamt of conquests as a suitor
And neglected his computer
(Were you his origins to seek
Would soon discover he was Greek)

A Travel Agent so superior
He worked for the *M.V. Illiria*,
And as his errors now attest
Was making out the manifest
And by the date of birth for Coker
Failed as a faultless keyboard stroker.

At the appointed place and line
In lieu of typing zero nine,
Our clumsy M attentive hero
Struck instead a nine and zero.
Thus engraved for all to see
An error by a century!

At Singapore we strained to view
Our passenger of ninety-two
But what to everyone's surprise
Should greet our sharp and prying eyes –
The Belle of Hartsville – E.B.C.
The Mother of Penelope.
"It <u>can't</u> be true!" the crowd all cried
This vicious rumor is denied
By flashing eyes and sparkling wit.
Besides we've read what she has writ.
For years we've watched as she composes
Works of art like <u>Blood Red Roses</u>.

So on her birthday we now cheer
Best wishes for another year.

You are a treat to have along
Taking part in dance and song
We toast you from the highest stupa
Our yellow bird of Larantuka.

Elizabeth delivered her own rhyme in response, unable to resist wielding her well-honed pen:

To round out my year of seventy-three
I went to test my Karma in far Bali.
But when I landed in Singapore
I discovered I'd added twenty more!
To top this off – to my amaze –
The Hindu year has 420 days.
Which brought my total to 106!
Has e'er poor girl been in such a fix?
Yes. Our bus guide, a handsome Hindu boy,
Announced with glee, yea, even joy,
That a human being you ain't not
When a human husband you ain't got.
But at the summit of Borobudur
I glimpsed the Nirvana I struggle for.

So grateful am I for this birthday roast,
And drink to all of you this toast:
As folks to tour with – you're the Most!

• • • • •

The following year, Elizabeth was back in Millbrook with Penelope and Eliza, researching the Sara Roosevelt biography at the FDR Library. It proved slow going at first, for as she complained, "Franklin's memory takes forever to function." Eventually they hammered out an outline and a working title – *Sara's Story: A Biography of Sara Delano Roosevelt*, as told by Franklin Delano Roosevelt, Jr., and Elizabeth Boatwright Coker.

Soon Elizabeth was confronted with another concern: the competition.

"Two recently published books [including Geoffrey Ward's *Before the Trumpet*] based on the same research that I have put together on Sara D., make a fresh approach obligatory," she revealed to a friend. "But since the end of summer, the new approach has begun to gather exciting momentum."

Elizabeth produced a draft manuscript by the end of 1986. As she began the process of querying publishers and calling on various agents and editors, two tragic events derailed the project. In June of 1987 Franklin, Jr., and his wife and son were thrown from a carriage he was driving on the family horse farm in Millbrook. Toby Roosevelt and young Jack were treated and released from the hospital. But Franklin, Jr., suffered a serious head injury that required surgery and cost him his left eye. He never fully recovered and fourteen months later died of lung cancer at the age of 74.

Elizabeth was devastated. She had lost another good friend. And now *Sara's Story* would be consigned to the archives. Like many successful authors, Elizabeth had produced several manuscripts over the years that, for one reason or another, were never published – including *Tyger, Tyger*, *The Way of an Eagle* and *Miss Elizabeth and the Yellow Corvette.* She was no stranger to disappointment. She knew how to pick herself up and carry on.

• • • • •

Wherever she landed, Elizabeth immersed herself in philanthropic and community endeavors. She became a trustee of the Pennsylvania Medical College and the National Advisory Council of International Social Service. She chaired the Pee Dee Heritage Center Advisory Board and served on the boards of the S.C. State Museum, the Palmetto Trust for Historic Preservation and the University of South Carolina Caroliniana Society. She was also a member of the Palmetto Garden Club and the Garden Club of America.

Her passion for education led her to serve for ten years on the Hartsville School Board. She enjoyed lecturing about the writing process to young elementary and high school students, and was a popular commencement speaker. She was also a member of the American Association of University Women and served as an associate visiting professor at Appalachian State University – not far from her mountain house in Blowing Rock.

Elizabeth guest-taught at Converse and Coker colleges, receiving honorary degrees from both. She was devoted to the two institutions and dedicated a great deal of time and energy to them. A lifetime trustee of Converse, Elizabeth adopted Coker as a second alma mater – never hesitating to aid either school any way she could.

In the early 1980s, she donated a large portion of her personal library to Converse. The college established the Elizabeth Boatwright Coker Visiting Writer program in her honor, hosting prominent authors such as Erin McGraw, Joyce Carol Oates, Jillian Weiss and Margaret Luongo.

In 1990, Elizabeth announced that she and Penelope and James, along with the Coker Foundation and other family interests, were donating a performing arts center to Coker College – "to honor and glorify" the institution "as well as the whole Pee Dee area." Upon completion, the auditorium was christened the Elizabeth Boatwright Coker Center for Performing Arts.

• • • • •

Elizabeth remained active and engaged in her final years. She was affiliated with many writers associations – including the Authors Guild, the National Academy of Poets, PEN International and the Poetry Society of South Carolina. She enjoyed listings in both Who's Who in America and Who's Who in the World. In 1991, at age 82, she was inducted into the South Carolina Academy of Authors, joining such other literary figures as James Dickey, Alice Childress, Pat Conroy, Louis Rubin, Julia Peterkin and DuBose Heyward. The Elizabeth Boatwright Coker Fellowship in Fiction and Elizabeth Boatwright Coker Student Prize in Fiction are awarded annually by the Academy.

In February of 1992, South Carolina's highest honor was bestowed on Elizabeth when she was inducted into the South Carolina Hall of Fame. Family members flew in from around the country for the event, including Penelope, James and Eliza. General William Westmoreland, a 1986 inductee, delivered the introduction to the celebrated author: "If you've never met Elizabeth Coker, you have missed a tremendous delight. That grand lady is like a breath of fresh air, a sparkling diamond and a comfortable shoe. I'm honored to be here paying tribute to this wonderful writer."

Elizabeth's niece, Ann Bacot Boatwright Igoe, was unable to attend the ceremony. Instead, she penned an eloquent tribute to her aunt:

> [Elizabeth Boatwright Coker's] achievements and generosity have truly brought honor and fame to South Carolina. Beyond that, she has loved this state more than anyone can imagine. She has loved it with the most intense pride and has served it with the deepest loyalty. Speak naught against South Carolina, lest you wish to meet with a scathing attack of brilliant language, a stout heart, iron facts, and fisticuffs if necessary. She takes seriously the responsibility and obligation of being one of South Carolina's most important people.
>
> She knows this state's history backwards and forwards, its dates and its people. She and her people have been an important part of this history. She knows the names of all the South Carolina trees, its shrubs, and its flowers. She knows its crops, the smell of tobacco and the feel of cotton. She recognizes the call of its birds. I would be surprised if anyone knew more about South Carolina than she does.
>
> She has participated happily and vigorously in the biggest state occasions and has not hesitated to deliver lectures to the students of the smallest rural schools. She has spoken to the Garden Club of America, and with the same enthusiasm and even more pride, to the garden club over in Darlington.
>
> It is not only the big things, the "head-line-who's-who" things that make her South Carolinian of the year, but also the 'big' things that she has done that have not made the news. Many a South Carolinian's dream has become a reality because of Elizabeth Boatwright Coker. Individuals have been able to participate in activities that they could never have afforded alone. They have been able to receive an education, take a special trip, study a particular subject, make a down payment, have an operation, wear the proper clothes – because of her generosity.

The distinguished Davidson College history professor Dr. Chalmers

Davidson wrote the following congratulatory note to Elizabeth on the announcement of her induction into the Hall of Fame:

> Dear Lib,
>
> A hundred years ago every South Carolina child in school was taught that William Gilmore Simms was a great author. Maybe a century hence they'll be learning the same thing about you.
>
> Authoress aside, you are a great South Carolinian and an ornament to the Palmetto State.
>
> How I wish we could be with you on February 7th. Age has been kinder to you than to most of your contemporaries. We can be with you only in spirit, and if you break into a Charleston, that's the spirit.
>
> Felicitations, Congratulations and Rejuvenation,
>
> Chalmers and Alice Davidson

Elizabeth was overjoyed by the outpouring and honored to be among fellow inductees who represented some of South Carolina's most prominent leaders, writers and artists over three centuries – notables such as Arthur Middleton, General Francis Marion, Charles Pinckney, Ann Pamela Cunningham, Archibald Rutledge, Dizzy Gillespie and Anna Hyatt Huntington. Her acceptance speech demonstrated gratitude for her home state and its citizens.

> If my late husband, James Lide Coker III, were here beside me this morning, my being inducted into the South Carolina Hall of Fame would mean as much to him as it does to me. We were both privileged in being South Carolinians, all the way back to those first hearty souls who waded ashore at Port Royal in the late 1600s.

South Carolina history has always fascinated me and it has been my delight and pride to tell of its glories and its sadnesses and its triumphs.

The past never totally fades for us. We may forget it, but we always hold it within ourselves. No one can ever be expected to write about it or to talk about his home state objectively for it is so much a part of the fabric of his mind and emotions that detachment is impossible. And I recall for the mere delight of recalling, happenings and people that I can never forget, treasures of my curious and secret heart . . .

It has often been difficult for me to break away from the realities around me in order to write. But I have, and that is why I have managed to be three different "me's:" corporate wife, doting mother, and closet writer . . .

By developing an innate sense of humor, I have gone smoothly through many situations that would have undone me had I tried to kick them over with criticism and caustic comments.

If we place the proper value on laughter, we learn to believe in tolerance, which in the end is my strongest credo. I believe in tolerance of races, of the weak ones, the different, and of those who have climbed higher than myself. As we achieve tolerance we will automatically achieve the better life, for we will see more of the qualities that are decent, generous and noble in men, and our faith in the principles of Christ will be easy and natural.

• • • • •

Elizabeth grew increasingly reflective, aware of the inevitability of change and loss that come with old age. In a letter to friends during a long, hot summer in Hartsville, she described her state of mind:

> I'm in a nostalgic humor. The heat has hovered between 98 to 103 degrees all week. My house is not air-conditioned (except for my boudoir!). I swim a lot. I read a lot too . . .
>
> What a summer this has been! Hot tortuous weeks were spent cutting down my beautiful camellias, tea olives and azaleas that formed the beauty of my landscaped garden.
>
> There are multitudinous farewells to such vital personnel as my big yellow cook of 14 years; my beauty parlor lady who had striven to straighten my fuzzy curls for the past 20 years; my doctor deciding to go into politics; the garbage man vanishing into a city service (now you have to push your own can all the way out onto the street once a week); my caretaker at Blowing Rock retiring because of age, leaving my place bereft inside and out; my beloved Charleston niece going far away to Maine; Pat Myrer, my literary agent, whisked off the scene by medicine men. Dutton sold, my editors scattered . . .

More and more she focused on her legacy, in particular, her vast archive – letters, journals, research notes, speeches, book reviews, interviews, manuscript drafts, contracts, newspaper clippings, etc. – over seven decades' worth of documents and memorabilia.

> My current excitement is trying to decide what I am going to do with my papers, scrapbooks, Kodak albums, etc. The Caroliniana Library at the University of South Carolina has requested the EBC Collection be placed there. Converse wants the scrapbooks, kept during my years as a student there . . . I've decided to toss all my memorabilia into one big box. Fate is decreeing that I spend my eternity in a file room in the basement of the South Caroliniana Library.

Each year in her memory, the Caroliniana Library confers an Elizabeth Boatwright Coker Research Fellowship grant on a deserving graduate student.

• • • • •

As long as she could, Elizabeth stayed busy, composing articles and stories, and winning prizes for pieces she wrote on request for "good causes." Three of her favorite causes were the communities of Darlington, Hartsville and Blowing Rock.

Of course, she adored her family, but also her would-be families – including the people who worked for her at Loblolly Hill, from which she never moved. The men and women she once called "servants" became friends and saviors in the latter years.

Elizabeth had loved and served her state of South Carolina, and it had readily loved her back. Her success in the cut-throat world of books and publishing was a feather in the *chapeau* of this unusual Southern woman. Her father, her Boatwright aunts, Jim, her teachers at St. John's High and Converse – they all had fiercely believed in her. She had received their loving support, and in turn, she had poured it out on others. She unabashedly referred to and wrote about matters of the heart, including her own.

Ironically though, Elizabeth never wanted to be remembered as a writer of "historical romance," often the purview of female fiction writers. She preferred the term "historical novel," which lent her work the gravitas it deserved – despite her weaving some of the most complex, colorful, romantic plots of the genre.

Elizabeth knew that matters of the heart were not just "women's work," and that love could not be confined to a superficial category like "romance." Ultimately love – receiving it and giving it – was the basis of her indefatigable strength and boundless tolerance, her "strongest credo."

The concluding paragraphs of the 1964 letter she wrote to Ann Head after cleaning out the attic of the family home in Hartsville perhaps best illustrate Elizabeth's penchant for candidly confronting the past while perpetually engaging with the moment.

> [Cleaning out] the attic has turned into a milestone. Up there has rested Miss Carrie's house (Jim's mother), Mamma's house, the Blowing Rock house, my toys and books and clothes of olden times, my children's things, Jim's things, and enough soot and dust and books, and newspapers and shoes and hats

and the entire file (unfiled, naturally) of FORTUNE magazine since Vol. 1! Not to speak of all of a defunct pithy mag called PARK EAST, [along with] COUNTRY LIFES, VOGUES, BAZAARS, YALE REVIEWS and all the other heavy mags in piles that would overflow my library if stingily stacked from floor to ceiling!

I have handled, looked at, remembered and dusted a thousand faded photographs, hundreds of framed fancy pictures, invitations, lares and penates, James' electric train, ready to run, on its full length tracks fastened on a huge plyboard area, three stuffed wardrobe trunks, six baby beds, ten chamber pots, and oh so many many bits and pieces and ornaments and necessities of a life . . .

It was a whole life I'd kept hoarding under the eaves of my house. It felt secure that way – the letters always up there waiting to be reread and the glittery party dresses and shiny slippers and the doll babies and the tiny little chamber pots and all the diplomas and P's divorce decree and more wedding bells and Jim's numerous high silk hats. He did so love to dress up.

After I'd got a path cleared, I fixed a chair and a table for writing content labels. Now everything is put away in patterned piles, neat and orderly. All the frivolous feathery dusty "mess" has gone away in three full truckloads – big trucks. It took four husky black men an afternoon to accomplish this. No ghosts linger. They are exorcised.

Downstairs all at once, everything is different too. For I am alone in this lovely house. Funny I never knew it before. Until this particular morning I don't think I have realized that that life, symbolized in the conglomeration that was up there in the attic, is over. Gone. Lived. I am free now to die before I wake or to go away and never come back. I am suspended and raw and full of frailty. I have a feeling I will blow with whatever wind comes – in whatever direction.

Fortunately it's a lovely sunny day – Spring is here. One always forgets what a mass of color comes in a burst of remembered fragrance.

• • • • •

It was August 23, 1993 and Elizabeth was at her mountain house in Blowing Rock, North Carolina. She had hosted a small supper party the previous evening. That morning she found herself waiting to say goodbye to son James and his wife, and hello to daughter Penelope, soon to arrive. What better way to pass the time than jumping jacks? So, there in her driveway, doing her favorite exercise, she suffered a stroke. An ambulance took her to Hartsville and Penelope and James followed. A week later (on September 1) she died at Byerly Hospital. She was 84.

Elizabeth is buried next to Jim in Hartsville's Magnolia Cemetery. She often remarked how she wanted her gravestone to be emblazoned with the words of a certain teenager who worked at the local supermarket. He saw her pull up one day in a canary yellow Corvette – Elizabeth's most cherished and signature possession. A pair of big fuzzy dice dangled from the rearview mirror as she screeched to a halt. After loading her groceries, the young man exclaimed, "Scratch off, Mama!"

In that spirit, though with a more somber tone, Elizabeth's gravestone is inscribed with the last two lines of a poem by her favorite poet, Edna St. Vincent Millay. In 1923, Millay wrote a tribute to the beautiful suffragist and labor lawyer, Inez Milholland. Milholland famously led the 1913 women's suffrage parade in Washington, D.C., dressed in a flowing white cloak and crown, and riding a white horse – not unlike our Hartsville heroine a half-century later, roaring through town in a yellow Corvette, daring the world to stop her.

"... Even now the silk is tugging at the staff:
Take up the song; forget the epitaph."

INDEX

— D —

— S —

— T —

— U —

— V —

— W —

— Y —

ABOUT THE AUTHORS

Penelope Coker Hall

Born in Hartsville, South Carolina, Penelope Coker Hall matriculated to Sarah Lawrence College and eventually settled in New York, becoming a writer and host for Metromedia's Channel Five TV show "The New Yorkers." Later at NBC, Hall worked as a co-producer of several TV specials, including "Vanishing 400" and "Debutante." During this time, she met and married film producer William Wilson and in 1968 their daughter, Eliza, was born. In 1972, Hall left the performing arts and embarked on a new marriage with widower Mortimer Hall of Millbrook, N.Y. Ensconced in Millbrook for 50 years, Hall served as editor of *Dutchess Magazine* while raising daughter Eliza as well as Morti's five young children, along with a bevy of horses and dogs. Hall is author of several children's books and the novel *Riding High* (under the pseudonym of Emily Brooks), written with former E.P. Dutton editor Ann La-Farge. Today, she divides her time between Charleston, S.C. and Millbrook.

Eliza Wilson Ingle

Eliza Wilson Ingle is a New York native with Southern roots. She earned her BA in Dance from Middlebury College, and after a brief stint in New York City, moved to Charleston where she became a Professor of Dance at the College of Charleston. In addition to teaching, Ingle has been a performer and choreographer with Anonymity Dance Company. A dance reviewer for *The Post and Courier* covering Spoleto Festival USA, as well as a contributor to *Charleston Magazine* and *Charleston City Paper*, and creator and co-host of "Just Imagine" – a radio program covering local cultural events and people – she stays tapped into the arts and believes, as her grandmother did, in the power of story. She thanks her husband and three grown daughters for their love, laughter and support.

Virginia Christian Beach

Virginia Christian Beach was born in Richmond, Virginia and earned a BA in English from the University of Virginia. From there she served as a Peace Corps volunteer in East Africa, after which she worked for Little, Brown Publishers in New York. Beach is the author of four books and a writer and editor for numerous publications and periodicals. She and her husband reside in Charleston, South Carolina where their two grown children were raised.